The Biggest Mistake I Never Made

How an Indiana boy gave up basketball to become a world-class volleyball player

By Lloy Ball as told to Blake Sebring

authorHOUSE®

AuthorHouse™
1663 Liberty Drive, Suite 200
Bloomington, IN 47403
www.authorhouse.com
Phone: 1-800-839-8640

First published by AuthorHouse 11/18/2008

ISBN: 978-1-4389-2907-1 (sc)

Printed in the United States of America
Bloomington, Indiana

This book is printed on acid-free paper.

Thanks to Sheryl Krieg, Betty Stein and Chad Ryan.

Cover photo by Chad Ryan.

This book is dedicated to Sarah Jane Ball, for all her sacrifice and patience. Thank you, Sarah, for being the love of my life. I also dedicate this book to the most precious gifts in my life, my children. Dyer and Mya, I've loved you from your first breath and cherish the role as your father. It is the most important thing in my life. You two are my greatest accomplishments. I love you.

I would like to thank the following people for making me the athlete, husband, father and overall man I am today.

* My Mother and Father, Sandy and Arnie, my sisters, Amy "Pearl" and Jana Rae, my Grandpa Ray, Grandpa Ball, Grandma Viv and Grandma Bert and all my cousins, aunts and uncles.

My brothers-in-law, Trent Brya and Capt. Jamie Uptgraph "Upty", and my awesome nieces and nephews, Jamison, Caden, Peyton and Callaway.

My best friends forever: Jay Miller, Lance Adams, Jim Stoltzfus, Greg Keller and Sean and Shane Gibson.

* Coaches that gave me their time and energy: Don Wickman, Gay Martin, Bill Neville, Rod Wilde, Rick Butler and of course, the best coach in the country, Arnie Ball.

Thanks to the Schlegel family for being my second family. Bless Aunt Mary.

* To other families who taught me how important family is: The Johnsons, Moores, Motts, Bruecks, Frankes, Gibsons and Roemkes.

Here are others who have touched my life. If I forgot anyone, please forgive me.

Cheeks and Roger, CJ, Loren Gerbert, Jay Goldsteyn, Tony Luhning, Fred Malcolm, Ethan Watts, Mike Price, Marc Evans, Tom Hoff and family. Tommy Walker, Steam, Riley Salmon and family, Bob Barrett, Butch and Dorothy Perchan, Roz Martin, Pastor Kaser and family, the Winklejons.

Also, a special "Grazie Mille" to my European friends: Luca Novi and family, Peitro Peia and family, Giango, Gardo, Bovo, Pippo, Luca Cantigalli, Bimbo, Roman, Alex, Jannis, Boco, Freddy, Mr. Uemastu, Nobu, Yagi and Pete.

A shout out to the lake gang: Steve, Les and baby Dane and baby Reed, Pat and Paige, Lewie, Woody, Matt and Amy and Scott and Sarah.

The doctors and medical staff who have kept me on the court for 15 years: Dr. Tasto, Dr. Pritchard, the OTC gang: Margie, Nick, Ed and Scherer. Also, thanks to Aaron Brock. Indiana Physical Therapy, especially Dave Kuhn.

And Foxy and Scott at IPFW.

FOREWARD

As one myself, I've always thought it was hypocritical for sportswriters to criticize and castigate Tony Stewart after he says something the slightest bit controversial. Of all people, shouldn't journalists cherish athletes who actually have an opinion on something and are willing to share it? Do we want boring, monotone players who only tell us what they think we want to hear? It certainly would make for boring, monotone stories that no one wants to read.

In an era when most athletes would not express an opinion of the greater world around them under threat of torture, Lloy Ball is refreshing. Over the 20 years I have covered his achievements, I've never had an interview with him where I had to pull quotes out of him whether it was in person, on the phone or by email half a world away. Lloy has never been shy about telling what he's thinking, and maybe more importantly for my work, what he is feeling after exhilarating wins and crushing losses. As a sportswriter who loves to write the conflict, passion and emotion of the people playing the games, he's a rare athlete to work with.

He's also a very good athlete. In 2008 he became the first American male to compete in four Olympic games in one of the major team sports. He has played more than 400 matches for the United States national men's team, a record, and no one has been the U.S. captain longer than his 10 years. He has become the first American to win championships in the three major European professional leagues, and was also named the most valuable player of the European Champions league, essentially the best league in the world. To follow that up he was named MVP of the 2008 World League before leading the U.S. to the Olympic gold medal in Beijing. He is recognized almost everywhere – except in his home country.

And even in his hometown, he still has people who are never shy about saying to this face they think he made a mistake by not playing basketball for Bobby Knight at Indiana University. He was still hearing it even as he prepared to play in his fourth Olympics -- hence the title for this book.

None of his amazing success has changed who he is. When Ball came home to Fort Wayne after the Olympics, more than 150 friends and family waiting to greet him at the airport. He thanked them for coming and then asked that they be patient until he got around to see all of them. For more than an hour he exchanged hugs and signed autographs and everyone of any age who wanted to was allowed to try on his medal -- including people waiting to board the upcoming flights. Often, he was so busy signing he didn't bother to keep track of where his medal was.

In some ways I envy him. He's so comfortable talking about what he believes and feels and rarely worries what others think of it. That doesn't mean he goes out of his way to be controversial or offensive like Terrell Owens or Dennis Rodman sometimes, but he's also not afraid to say what he thinks. If you ask, you're going to get a heartfelt answer so you better be prepared to hear it. He'll also listen to what you think when he's finished.

With that kind of outlook on life, it's a good thing Lloy is an athlete because he could never get elected to political office. He's too open, too honest and too true to himself and his values. Heaven forbid.

We need more athletes and politicians like that, but our society in the form of agents and handlers beats individualism out of them very quickly. We need more athletes like Charles Barkley, Tony Stewart and Lloy Ball. At least when they speak, you know they believe what they are saying and no one else told them to say it. I fear they are becoming a dying breed.

Blake Sebring

Fort Wayne, Indiana

October 2008

CHAPTER 1

When I think of the national anthem and the Pledge of Allegiance, I realize my generation may be the last where these were taught in school. We had to stand every morning to say the Pledge of Allegiance.

From the get-go we've always been a pretty patriotic family. I remember every day helping my father put the flag up, and every night taking the flag down before sundown, not really knowing the importance of it other than I couldn't let it touch the ground for some reason. Otherwise all heck would break loose.

That symbol in our household, as soon as I could remember, was a very important symbol and everything that went with it, the Pledge of Allegiance to the National Anthem, to wearing the patch on your uniform. As far as singing the national anthem, it was always a song that kind of raised the hairs on the back of my neck, even from a young age and even though I really didn't know why.

I didn't know all the things my family had done as far as our military and fighting in wars, but as I began to go to college, I began to grow closer to my grandmother and grandfather. My grandfather Lloyd was pretty close-mouthed about his military experiences in World War II and about fighting for our country until later in his years after he retired from farming. Grandma, of course, never hid much of anything about the way she felt. One time at an IPFW game my freshman year, I remember looking into the stands during the national anthem and seeing my grandmother, who at that time was in her early 70s, singing this song as if it could be the last breath coming out of her 100-pound body and how focused she was. Everybody else was milling around, older people were taking the song more seriously, some of the college kids were still talking during it, but I was seriously taken aback by watching her.

The next time I was at grandma's and grandpa's, I asked Grandma, ``Why, why so emphatically?" And that's how the story began as far as her and Grandpa explaining to me the hardships of him being overseas and him being at Normandy. My grandfather was in one of only three Allied tanks out of 31 that survived D-Day. Then they talked about why the national anthem is so very important to them where maybe some other generations have lost that.

From that moment on, I decided I was going to sing it.

My grandfather was buried at Arlington National Cemetery in May, 2007, and, because I was playing in Russia when it happened, I wasn't able to attend. I recently watched the funeral video for the first time, with Grandma. My sister Amy's husband, Jamie Uptgraft is a captain with the 82nd Airborne, and that was the first time I had gotten to see Jamie's eulogy. As if I didn't appreciate him for everything he has done for my sister and our family, watching that made me appreciate him even more. He put into words what everyone in our family felt about the service Grandpa had done.

Grandpa had a bronze star, a Purple Heart, and they don't just put anybody into Arlington. To see the way they folded that flag and handed it to Grandma... To see the respect of the 21-gun salute, and to hear the Army Pastor say, ``This country can never repay the debt your husband has given."

Jamie will be there one day. He's had two tours in Iraq, and every day he gets a call that someone else in his command has died.

He's not my brother-in-law, he's my brother. He's a son to Dad, not a son-in-law. With the patriotism our family has, you couldn't ask for a better guy to join it. After two tours in Iraq, he's still with us and I have no doubt if he got called, he'd go again. He's a much stronger man than I could ever be. As patriotic as I am, to know that any moment could be your last just because of what you believe in your country... What he stands in front of dwarfs what I stand in front of with a ball. A ball hurts sometimes but that's about it. I know my sister probably

2

still believes that I love him more than I love her, and I tell her, ``You're right, but in a different way.'' Our family is just real lucky to have him be a part of us, not only because of what he has done for the country, but what he has done for our family.

For those of us who are not soldiers, I think it's real hard to put ourselves in Grandpa's shoes, or Jamie's shoes, and if you can, even for a moment, it makes you feel very fortunate to have people as extraordinary as Jamie and for sure my grandfather who basically are willing to give their lives so that all of us didn't have to. I always think of the equation that God gave Jesus so that we wouldn't have to, and obviously that's a much bigger pedestal, but it's kind of along the same lines for me when I think about what Grandpa did and what Jamie does.

I was watching a video Grandpa made a few years ago recently, and he said, ``We didn't know what we were getting into, we just knew this is what we were supposed to do and what we wanted to do.'' It's as simple as that. People like me who think they kind of know the world and have it by the tail… thinking about what he said makes me feel real small. Just being able to sing the national anthem on his behalf, and Jamie's behalf, and every other soldier for what they have done is the least we non-fighting Americans can do. It's the very least we can do to show our respect to them.

It's amazing, but every time I sing the anthem, it's almost like a drug. I feel better. I become so addicted, that half the time I kind of forget where I'm at, whether it's the Olympics or I'm in Greece or in Russia. During the song, I really couldn't tell you. I just focus on the words and how amazing it makes me feel and how proud it makes me feel to No. 1, be an American, and No. 2, to have so many great people in our family who have served our country to give us the freedoms and pleasures that we unfortunately take for granted today.

I just told myself I was going to sing it every time. Now I've played thousands of matches in dozens of countries and in four Olympics. It's by far the best thing I do. Having those three letters on my chest, it's not fighting in a war, it's not what Grandpa did or what Jamie Uptgraft does, but it's my way of representing my country. That's why when I play I give 100 percent, and when I'm overseas I try not to be too much of an American jerk. I'm real proud of that.

CHAPTER 2

Having heard a little of our family history, you can imagine how I felt when first putting on the uniform of our country. The first time I put on a USA uniform was when coach Bill Neville took me out of Woodlan High School back in 1988 for a trip to Japan. Scott Fortune broke his leg, they needed a guy and all the college kids were playing, so he said this is a great chance to give this young kid a taste.

My dad called me at school and I remember getting called down to the principal's office which is never a good thing. Luckily, I didn't spend much time there in high school. I come in and the vice principal says, ``Your dad is on the phone."

The first words out of Dad's mouth are, ``Do you want to go to Japan?"

"What are you talking about?"

``Bill Neville called and they need a guy and I have to let them know today. I'll take you out of school for 10 days and you'll go to play with the national team."

I couldn't even process this so I just said yes. Luckily, being 17, I couldn't get my head around it. Of course later that night when we got home and Dad started to explain it to me, I was just like, it's basically flying 20 hours to a place I've never been to play with a team I know that I'm really not good enough to be on.

``No, I changed my mind."

Dad was like, ``No, they already sent the ticket," and I was leaving the next day.

I was pretty adamant to Mom and Dad. Once I started thinking about it, I realized I had no business being on this trip. I had the straight tourist thing going on.

He was like, ``Obviously, Coach Neville sees something in you that he thinks can help or benefit the team.''

I'm just thinking, ``You're just lying to make me feel good'' because he and I both knew Dad had a better chance at helping the team than I did by playing.

Dad just said, ``I think they want to show you what your future could be. Don't take it so much as a tryout. You're not going to make or break your career with this trip. You probably aren't even going to play. This is just a chance that Coach Neville is giving you to see what your future could be. You kind of know what basketball could be, but you've never really seen what international volleyball at the highest level with the travel and everything, the good and the bad, is like. This is more of chance to glimpse what your future might be.''

I tried to think of it that way, but I was still nervous. The first day we were playing pepper, a passing game, I think I missed every ball.

The next morning the first flight out of Fort Wayne was around 6 a.m. across to Chicago and from Chicago to Los Angeles where I met the team. I finally saw a friendly face in Bill Neville because I really didn't know any of the guys. He's basically the one who got me started in the national program in volleyball, getting me into the Olympic Festival to get my feet wet when I was 15.

I had never flown anywhere near that length. I remember we're sitting in coach and in front of me was Allen Allen who is a big, 6-5 Hawaiian man, and he had his seat all the way back. I was still 6-8 at this time. I remember it was a 12-hour flight and I didn't sleep at all. I was just nervous and this and that, and he's basically in my lap the whole way. I can't go back because one of the other guys from the team is sitting behind me and he won't let me put my seat back, so I'm essentially sitting upright for 12 hours with Allen breathing on me from one side and another guy from behind, but I really didn't mind. I think I had a tape recorder and headphones at the time. I put that on and listened to some Bon Jovi and was just excited about going to Japan.

We were in Japan, and here I am, everyone else is mid-20s and 30s, and I'm 17. I had no idea what the heck I was doing, except I'm carrying everybody's bags. They gave me the ice bucket, which I thought was no big deal, except I had a big block of ice that I had to chip with my own hands and carry it about seven blocks through downtown Tokyo to the arena. Finally, Javier Gaspar helped me out. At that time I was 6-8 and 180 pounds and I could barely carry my own bags, much less this big ice chest.

We got to the game and I had yet to get a uniform. I thought maybe I was just here to play pepper or carry the ice bag all the way through Japan. We get to the game and everybody has their uniform on and all of a sudden Coach Neville comes over and says, ``Well, here it is, are you ready? Here's your uniform. Before you take it out of the bag, I want you to know there's a lot of pressure going into wearing this uniform, not only because of what's on it in the front, but also on the back.''

I open it up and of course there's big red letters USA on the front and on the back No. 15, which was Karch Kiraly's number. Last time they saw No. 15 on the USA team was the year before when Karch was still playing because he had just retired. So not only was there pressure to represent my country, but also pressure to wear No. 15.

I was kind of hoping I wouldn't play so I wouldn't let anybody down.

We walked onto the court in Osaka, and there are 20,000 people. I had never seen that many people at anything, especially a volleyball game, and here I am wearing USA, singing the national anthem and standing next to guys like Bob Ctvrtlik, Rod Wilde, Steve Timmons, Adam Johnson – guys that I had only seen on TV. Then you throw in the fact that you have USA on your shirt, playing in a place where no more than 30 to 40 years ago the people weren't too happy with us, and it was just an overwhelming first experience.

I think I slept maybe an hour a night the whole trip because I was so excited. I looked out the hotel window most nights at all the signs, or went down to try to get a Coke out of a machine I couldn't understand. It was just overwhelming. Talk about cultural shock, it's one thing when high school kids go down to Tijuana or someplace like that, but here's a kid from Woodburn which is middle-American and 2,300 people who are good hard-working folks, and my first cultural experience is Japan.

It was also like a drug. That's how I describe a lot of things in volleyball, such as why I'm still playing. I see why rock stars like to be rock stars. You are singing in front of thousands and thousands of people. It's just an adrenalin rush, and that's what it felt like. To represent something as big and powerful as the United States of America, it's a bit overwhelming for a 17-year-old kid from Woodburn.

It was a four-match series, the last match we're losing 0-2. Japan was real good at this time, and we were in kind of a transitional stage with the team after a lot of guys had left following the 1988 Olympics. So we're losing 0-2 and 12-10 in the third game when Coach Neville comes back and says, ``It's your time.''

I'm like, for what?

``You're going in.''

Right there I can't feel my legs. I somehow managed to walk up to the scorer's table, and he hands me a substitution paddle which, of course, I drop it. I get to the sideline and he's calling Rod Wilde to come out of the game, and Rod said, ``Who's going to set?'' and I'm standing right there in front of him. That's how much confidence Rod Wilde had in me for my first experience.

I go in and luckily we're serving. I actually went to serve, and I probably put in the easiest float serve that you've ever seen, probably about 30 feet high over the net, right into the middle of the court. It was just a lollipop. Somehow we get a block, and then we scored another point to tie it up 12-12. Then we have to side out and this is my first sideout attempt, and I'm looking around going there's no way I'm going to try to set a quick because I'll probably set it underneath the net. I'm not real confident with setting the ball backwards right now, either. I look over and there's Ctvrtlik on the left side, Good option! The first set I send Ctvrtlik is probably about six feet past the antenna. Un-hittable,

8

so it's 13-12. Nobody is laughing. The guys are all serious, they are semi PO'd that I'm in there.

So the next set, a real good pass, so I'm thinking that didn't work so let's try a little bit shorter distance. Don Denninger was playing middle so I set him a quick, and of course the Japanese team knows what's going on and that I'm a young guy and I'm nervous, so they have this 6-6 guy totally committing block, and I set the ball about three inches above the net and he gets housed straight down. There's 14-12, so it doesn't look too good. So it's my last chance, I'm in the back row so I can't tip, so I said I was going to set Ctvrtlik one more time. I actually set him a good ball, but now there were actually three blockers out there because they knew there was nowhere else I was going, and he gets blocked and we lose.

That was my first international experience, siding out at 0 percent and not doing too well.

The guys didn't say anything because they were a little peeved at coach right after, I think. That night as we were on the bus ride to the airport for the flight home, some of them came to me because they had seen me practice throughout that whole week. They just said, ``Hey you are a nice prospect, just keep working," and that kind of thing. They were real supportive, but in the end all of those guys, they are just so competitive that they probably would have liked to kill me on the court. Later that night they were real cool about it.

After that last match, let's just say I wasn't real sure about my future with USA Volleyball.

Coach Neville was the first one to come up and say, ``You did fine. It was an unbelievable situation to put you in and we just wanted to get you some kind of experience and idea of what the travel is like and what it's like playing with jet lag and sleeping in beds that are four foot long."

I was pretty jazzed anyway, but looking back, the hardest part about playing overseas is that kind of trip.

I remember coming home and I think I didn't go to school the next day so I could sleep all day. The reaction around school was kind of half and half. Half of the people who liked me thought I was a rock star because there was something in the paper about it, and I'm sure I wore some kind of Japanese ensemble that I purchased there and I was telling stories about everything. Some people thought I was kind of a jerk because they thought I was a jerk before. It was kind of 50-50. Most of my friends were super jazzed because I know I spent more time the next week telling stories than I did doing homework.

Besides having a volleyball coach for a father, that experience was probably the No. 1 reason I played USA volleyball for 15 years. Coach Neville is obviously an intelligent man. He knew me well enough and knew how much I was like my father that if I got it in my blood, I'd have a hard time getting it out.

CHAPTER 3

Putting on the USA uniform still feels the same today. As I was trying to decide whether to play for the USA in the Beijing Olympics, the over-riding factor was how I feel when I put it on. From the very first time I put it on until the last time as of this moment that I took it off in Athens, I feel invincible. I feel like 300 million people are supporting me. I feel like I'm guessing George Bush feels when he walks into a room full of Republicans. It makes you jump higher, it makes you play harder, it makes you do things you didn't think you could.

People ask me all the time what it feels like to put the uniform on, and I say, ``It always fits." Even if it's XXXL or a small, it always fits. It always feels good and it's always an honor to wear it.

It's like a pair of pants you just can't throw away. It becomes part of you. My wife yells at me because I like to wear them out and around, not to show off, but because I love the way I feel in them.

I probably have given away over 500 during my career, but I keep one of every color and style that I have ever received. From the No. 15 all the way to the last one I wore in Athens. I've probably got 36 to 40 different ones. They are all different every year with different styles and different sponsors, and Olympic jerseys are different from normal jerseys. My favorites are the old ones. Now every country has just the little flag on their right chest with their name. My favorite is the Olympic one from 1996. That's when they could still put USA on it in big letters across the front.

I must get a request from somebody once a month asking for a jersey for this or that. We do a lot of charities, and a lot of volleyball fans just like to put them up. If family or friends have a good cause or a charity,

I have no problem giving them one for that. A lot of them have gone to auctions to help Dad's program.

They are pretty cool. Any time you can get an Olympic jersey from any sport, they are pretty rare. I haven't seen too many on eBay come across so luckily nobody is selling them.

One thing I get on the young guys about is treating the uniform with respect. As long as it says USA Volleyball on the front, it's tucked in, even if it's just a polo shirt we're traveling in. I don't wear a dirty one. When they used to have all the uniforms in one sack and one guy washed them, I always kept mine out and kept it with me because I wanted to make sure it was there when I needed it, and that it was kept clean. It's kind of like the flag. You don't wipe up sweat with it, and you don't just throw it in a bag. You treat it with the kind of respect you'd treat the flag with because it's kind of an extension of that.

I got to have a very special experience on July 4, 2004. As part of an Olympic-preparation tour, we were playing Brazil in Fort Wayne in the Allen County War Memorial Coliseum. Normally people who come to the games always have some kind of red, white and blue on to show their support, but that day there wasn't a soul without red, white and blue on. To play on Independence Day in a place like Fort Wayne where it still means something was amazing. Unfortunately in some places in our country, it has lost some of that luster, but being a very proud and mostly Republican area, the Fourth of July is a pretty big thing there. To represent our country on a day like that is a pretty big thing. I'm guessing it's sort of like a soldier getting to march in a parade. That's kind of my exhibition for my country. It was a real special feeling.

CHAPTER 4

I was born February 17, 1972 in Parkview Hospital in Fort Wayne. I was 10 pounds, 4 ounces and 25 inches long – just a big boy. My mom always says the first time she saw me this big African American nurse came in, and Mom said she probably weighed 200 pounds, just a big lovely, happy lady. She comes in holding this big baby, she smiles and lays me on my mom and says, ``Now this is my kind of baby. A big ol' baby."

I grew up in a small house in rural Indiana, with a school teacher dad who also coached three or four different teams. Mom quit her job to stay home when she started having us. It was kind of a ``Leave It to Beaver" household, you know, where Dad works but is an attentive dad, and Mom is the loving, supportive one, a taking care of scraped knees kind of Mom.

There was no fighting. I always tell people this today and nobody believes it, but it's one of the reasons my marriage is so good. I never saw my parents fight. Never. I never saw my father raise his voice, I never saw my mom cry. I don't know if it happened or not, but I never saw it and I lived at home 18 years, and my sisters will say the exact same thing. Either they faked it real well or we were very lucky to have such a great example, and I know exactly which one it is. We had a great example for parents, and I think that's a reason why my sisters and I have great relationships with our spouses.

It was just a great place to grow up. We had seven country acres, backing up to a river. It was a ranch, but there no animals. We lived by U.S. 24, and my mom and dad never let us have any pets because of semis on the highway. I just spent a lot of time climbing buckeye trees, trying to find muskrats down by the river, fishing, riding bikes in the grass and of course playing as much basketball as any Indiana boy could play using a backboard that my dad and I made.

My Mom is the unsung hero in our family, the glue that keeps all us crazy ones together. She drove us kids all over creation, stayed up late when we were sick, made sure we had homemade food on the table every night, and she was the one we all went to with our problems. I never gave my mom enough credit through the years. And I should have.

My sisters Amy and Jana are classic chicks. They are as different as day and night, but they are best friends. I have stayed very close with them, even though I was out of the house by the time they hit high school. My sisters are probably the only people who really understood me. They weren't fooled too much my silliness. They knew that I was a decent guy inside, even though I tried to prove them wrong.

They were put into a tough spot, my being their brother, either because of my accomplishments, or because of me making an ass out of myself. I know sometimes that they disliked me and defended me all in the same day. They are beautiful, accomplished women, great examples of what a young woman should be. And I am proud to be their brother.

I was always in the 90th percentile of my height, but nothing crazy. I started eighth grade at 5-7 which was normal. I started freshman year at 6-4, I started my sophomore year at 6-8 and then I was done. Dad tells me that it comes from his side of the family, and I'm not sure I believe him or not. He's maybe 5-10 when he's got his platforms on. Mom is about 5-9. I guess it's in the Ball family, looking at all of Grandma's brothers down in Tennessee. We went down and met them a bunch of times for Thanksgivings and such, and they're all 6-6, 6-7. It just happened to skip my dad and his brothers and sisters. My sister Jana is almost 6-0, and I have two cousins who are 6-4.

I tried to play all the sports growing up, but I just wasn't very good. I'm still not real coordinated but back then I wasn't very coordinated at all. I couldn't jump, wasn't fast and was real weak. When I was 6-8 my sophomore year, I only weighed 180 pounds. I'm 6-8 now and 235.

Growing up I played baseball, and I loved baseball because my dad loved baseball. I tried to play soccer and I was the goalie. I could barely kick the ball 20 yards, and I remember in my eighth grade year they scored two goals on me between my legs. That ended that career.

I played tackle football one year. I was kind of a wuss and didn't like it. I played baseball for one year.

Basketball just seemed to be a natural fit. I was big and had good hands because my dad started me playing volleyball at a young age. Even when I was very young, I saw the court real well. People always thought I was something of a wuss for not playing in the paint, but I was always more comfortable seeing everything like I do in volleyball. I was kind of a point guard/two guard because it was easier for me. I saw lanes and saw guys cutting, just like in volleyball I can see guys jumping. It was kind of a natural fit for me. Eventually, by the time I reached high school, I just played basketball and volleyball.

Volleyball really started when I was four years old playing on the carpet in our living room. Dad would build the pillows up like a net, and he and I would play one-on-one with a balloon. And then I did it with my sisters. For some reason, it didn't take with them, probably because I kept spiking the balloon in their face. I always tell kids that story in camps, and people think I'm making it up but I remember that.

I also couldn't have been much more than six or seven years old, rolling the ball up on our shed roof and when it would roll down, bumping it back up. As mundane and boring as that sounds, I'd do it for hours. I'd go outside in the wintertime wearing my Mom's gloves, shooting baskets in the snow for an hour and then I'd go set the ball against the garage door for an hour, just in my winter boots and gloves. I just always liked playing ball. Growing up out in the country and not having any brothers, I was always pretty good at entertaining myself, finding a way to do things.

My father never pushed any sports on me. People always tell me I'm lucky because I had a dad who pushed and drove me, and I try to tell them that my dad could have cared less. He wanted me to play, but he was never going to force his will. I think if I had been great in school and had become a doctor he would have been really, really happy. I know how hard he worked, and he just wanted his kids to be successful. One of my sisters is successful at Disney World and my dad loves it. One wrote a children's book and my dad loves it. I just think he wants his kids to be happy and successful and that's all.

I think it was a perk that I chose sports and a bigger one that it was volleyball, but, I think, if anything his effect wasn't pushing me but I spent a lot of time growing up with him. I remember when he coached at Harding High School and the Saturday morning trips to tournaments when he coached the IPFW men's and women's teams. I've been to every IPFW volleyball camp since 1984, either participating or instructing. It was part of my life, part of my lifestyle even before I had a lifestyle, and the volleyball lifestyle just fits me. I'm a very social person. I like to talk, I like to have a beverage after games with teammates and fans, and I love to entertain, just like my old man does.

Volleyball was a club sport in high school so I played for a limited time, basically just in the spring and summertime. Once the basketball season was over, Dad would always start a club team for me to play on, and it was basketball guys or guys who didn't play baseball and wanted something to do. It was basically 12 country kids and me, and none of them had any idea about volleyball except what Dad or I tried to get them to do, but it was great. It was a chance for me to play. We always went to Chicago for the Junior Olympics or we'd go to tournaments in Muncie.

Those guys got excited about the tournaments because there were about 300 girls teams there. In high school, and that was right up their alley. I talk to those guys when I see them now, and they had a great time and we have some good memories. Dad did a nice job of supporting me and finding me a place to play.

I was an unmotivated student. I was smart enough to know what I had to do. I knew my parents would not let me play sports if I didn't do well enough. At the same time, I was happy with a B. My sisters always had to have A's. For me, it didn't make much difference.

Hopefully my kids as students are more like my sisters. My wife and I both got through college, but I think she'd agree that was not the top priority for either of us because we both played sports, and both were somewhat social. I don't think we'll put extra pressure on them to be better because we weren't. My goal is for my kids to do the best they can. That's all my Mom and Dad wanted out of us.

I think my kid is an unbelievably well-adjusted five-year-old considering he's lived in Europe more than he's lived in this country. He's had experiences that most people who are 50 years old have never had. I think that's going to give him a great advantage over other kids his age. Will he be great at reading and writing, great at math and chemistry? I don't know and only time will tell, but I know Sarah and I are very adamant that it's not just the teachers' responsibility to teach my children. It's my responsibility. When they come home and have homework, I'll sit there and help them through it. I have a huge problem with people who want me, Michael Jordan and Barry Bonds to be role models. That's not an athlete's job. That's the only thing I agree with Charles Barkley on. That's my job as a parent. I'm the role model for my kid. It's my job to make sure he turns out good. If he doesn't turn out good, there's only one person I'm going to blame, and that's myself.

CHAPTER 5

Coming into my senior year of high school, our basketball team was picked to finish in the top 10 in the state. Jim Mosher and I were junior all-staters the year before and we had a great team coming in. Everyone on our team was over 6-0 and Jim was 6-4. We were real athletic.

I had a nice senior season, averaging 20 points and 10 rebounds per game, along with three blocked shots and three or four assists per game. The knock on me was I didn't play in a real tough conference, and usually when we got a little further in the state tournament we had to play a Fort Wayne school like North Side or a South Side who played a little different tempo than we did, and we struggled. So nobody knew how good I really was, and I really didn't know either. I'm the leading scorer in Woodlan history with 1,267 points, but I'm not really sure that means that much.

It was only after my senior season that I started to get a lot of recruiting letters. I went down to the Top 40 workout in Indianapolis and I was just dunking on the Ross boys who later went to Notre Dame, and throwing up threes, and then we had the Indiana North vs. South game, and it was me and the guys from up here against Damon Bailey, Eric Montross and the gang. We just worked them over as I scored something like 27 points. I really came into my own after the season, probably because I got a little bit bigger, stronger and more coordinated, and I had a lot of confidence all of a sudden. Then we had the Indiana All Stars against the Russians at the Memorial Coliseum. I played five minutes and scored 11 points.

After that, things really started to happen. Louisville called, Kentucky, Purdue, IU, USC wanted me bad to play both basketball and volleyball. Stanford wanted me bad to play both. I had already decided from the get-go, if I was going to play basketball, I wanted to play at IU, and if I was going to play volleyball, I was going to play for my dad at Indiana-Purdue Fort Wayne. Those were the choices I made. IU was the only recruiting trip I took.

I grew up liking Purdue and that's where I wanted to play growing up. I remember watching the IU-Purdue games on TV, and I knew my dad, as an IPFW coach, was paid by Purdue while everyone else loved IU, so of course I cheered for the other team. My high school coach tried to get Purdue's Gene Keady to look at me, but they weren't too interested. I really only talked to a few coaches, but I decided early on that I didn't want to fly around looking at tons of schools.

I narrowed it to IU because they were the best at that time, and Coach Knight was a legend. I had played with his son Pat, and everyone and their mother was telling me IU was the best choice. I liked the fact that it was nearby, and that many people from our area went to school there. My high school girlfriend was going to go there as well, so it seemed like an easy fit.

But it was an excruciating decision, really the only hard thing I'd had to do with my life up until that moment because I was so torn. Every day at school I've got secretaries, teachers, friends and people who didn't even like me for four years telling me I had to go to IU. Most of the kids from my high school went to IU, and most of the staff had graduated from down there so it was a big IU place. Obviously everyone supported Coach Knight and that program and it was just relentless. I'd find notes in my locker saying, ``Go to IU.'' Girls who would never even think about dating me would say, ``Hey, I'm going there next year. Maybe you and I could date.'' It was kind of like rock stars type stuff. Teachers who I had to beg for B-minuses were asking if I needed extra help in school or tutoring and things like that to prepare for SATs. I went from being a good athlete and people knew me to sort of like the class president for a while.

The other thing was, who from Woodlan ever gets a scholarship to IU? Nobody. And then I've got guys from volleyball like Bill Neville telling me I should pick volleyball – in Sports Illustrated.

Meanwhile at home where I'm looking for help, I've got nothing. I've got Mom making me dinner and Dad making no comment. He would not say anything about it until the night before. I was back and forth and I didn't know what to do. We had a press conference scheduled in the school gym and it was going to be on TV, and 24 hours before I still had no idea which way I was going to go.

Meeting Coach Bob Knight was something. It was an open gym at the end of my senior year, right before graduation. He comes up with assistant coach Ron Felling and he immediately goes to the corner of the gym up in the bleachers. My dad goes up there to talk to him, our Athletic Director Elmer Strautman goes up there and Knight never even says hello to me.

Every Tuesday and Thursday, Gay Martin, my high school basketball coach, held open gym from 7 to 9 p.m. It was guys like myself who maybe were finished and were about to graduate, underclassmen and people always came back to play. It was maybe 40 guys on three courts and you play, ``Winner stays." Coach Martin always kind of put the teams together, and he always put five guys who might be the five for next year together so they could start playing together. Guys like me who were done with high school would play with the older guys and try to rip them apart.

We start playing and the whole time Ron Felling is just walking up and down the court watching, not saying anything, just watching. He never even looks at Coach Knight. It turns out Knight is up there telling history stories, and they're not even talking about basketball. I don't know what the heck they are doing.

I think people look at Coach Knight like he's Caesar or Czar Ivan, but I didn't find him arrogant or abusive. He was very sure about everything he said, never showing indifference and he is one of the most intelligent people I have ever met. He has a lot of confidence. I still have the utmost respect for him, and I believe that he is one of the greatest coaches in history and cares very much for his players.

It was funny because the only other guy who played well that night was Marc Evans who was a heck of an athlete. Some of the other guys were kind of nervous and it was sort of clanksville and stuff. It didn't bother me to play in front of him because for one thing he wasn't paying attention, and I wasn't even sure I thought the whole thing was serious.

It was interesting because after we get done, usually we all sit in the stands and talk or go down and shower or talk about if we were going to do anything that night. Everyone went down to the locker room that night and there was absolute silence. Everybody is looking at me and I'm looking around shrugging my shoulders. Finally, after about 10 minutes, I'm like, ``Did I play good?" I couldn't even remember. Then we started talking, and somebody said, ``I don't even think Coach Knight was even looking at us." All of a sudden we picked up the dialogue and stuff, but we were pretty nervous talking about it.

After we're done, and I go to shower and come out, Ron Felling comes up and says, ``Yes, I like what I see." He pointed out some really non-specific things to me like one time an offensive rebound came out and I tipped it to a guy under the basket for an assist and he made it. They were random little things that didn't have anything to do with shooting or rebounding, but more how I was seeing the game, passing and ball-handling.

We walk down to the end and Coach Knight comes up, shakes my hand and he sits down. He really didn't talk to me, he talked around me to everybody else. It maybe lasted15 minutes because it was pretty much all talked about before I got there between Elmer Strautman, my dad and him. He's blunt. ``If you play basketball, I think you should play for us. Let us know." He told me not to come to IU with any preconceived notions, and that he would make me into whatever he wanted. And that was it.

A week later they sent a plane up and I made a recruiting trip and away we went. That was awesome. I show up at Baer Field and there's a plane sitting there with a big IU on the tail. I walk on and there are these big first-class seats with two retired pilots flying it. I'm the only guy on the plane and the stewardess is serving me sandwiches and Coca-Colas. I get down there, and I've been on IPFW's campus since I was a baby, but this is my first time to actually be on a Big Ten campus. It's huge and there are millions of people. And they all know I'm the new recruit. Every girl comes up and says ``You have to come here," and every guy says, ``You have to come help us win the national championship." I don't know if they knew me or not, or if they had handed out a flyer before I got there that said ``If you see this man, stop him."

We go down and meet a counselor. What do you want to major in? Communications. Here's your schedule. Boom just like that. Who do you want to room with? I had become good friends with Pat Knight, and, ``He said he likes you, too, so here's your apartment key." It was done, it was over. All I had to do was sign and I'd be in class three months later.

The experience was a little overwhelming actually, but awesome. It made it real hard to say no.

CHAPTER 6

The end of school was coming, and everyone wanted to know what I was going to do, including me. So, after Coach Martin, Mom and Dad and I decided it was between IU and IPFW, I had two weeks to decide before we would have a press conference.

It was the worst two weeks of my life. Everyone from friends to my girlfriend's father was telling me to go to IU. My parents were the best, never pushing me one way or the other. My one or two close friends, Jay and Marc didn't, either.

All this time I'm not sleeping a whole lot, except in class. It seemed like everything that made sense was on the IU side, but when we sat at the kitchen table after dinner the night before the press conference, my parents sent the girls to their room. Mom said, ``What are you going to do?"

``What do you think I should do?"

``Whatever makes you happy."

So I say, ``All right, Dad, you haven't said anything in this whole process. What should I do?"

He says, ``I think you would be crazy not to go play for Coach Knight."

Not what I was expecting at all.

And that was the end of the conversation. I got up and went to my room and lay there all night.

I got up the next morning and knew what I was going to do. I had replayed it all in my head. I always say the same prayer every night before I go to bed, and if there's some extra stuff I throw that on at the end. The ending to that one was probably another five minutes, the ``give me a sign" kind of prayer. I never got a sign, but I just woke up the next morning after about an hour's sleep, and I just knew.

I didn't tell anybody. I probably said three words all day. I didn't sit with my normal crowd at lunch. I got a bunch of passes from Coach Martin to hide out in his office. I just tried to keep away because I was so sure I just didn't want to hear any more.

I got to the press conference after school and Dad comes up, ``You know what you are going to say?" I just kind of put my hand on his shoulder and said, ``I want to play for you."

It was awkward but he didn't say anything. He just nodded his head.

To some moans and groans, I said, ``I'm going to sign with IPFW." I'll bet there were 100 to 150 people there in the gymnasium, including all the teachers.

To this day, people ask me if I could have that moment back, would I take it back? Never.

Everybody was pretty low, pretty disappointed in me. I was really glad that school was just about over because no one was real pleased with my choice. There were a lot of rumors after that day. I wasn't that well liked in high school anyway, so this just kind of added to it. Woodlan is a big IU school so people were ticked. I'm sure they were all thinking free tickets to Bloomington and maybe we'll know an NBA guy if he does well. I was happy that was over.

I obviously put a lot of thought into the decision. You know when something has been part of your life for so long that maybe sometimes you can't even describe it, but it just becomes part of you? Volleyball over the years had become part of me, being in every gym in Indiana, seeing my father coach men and women in high school and college, watching and getting so excited to see the U.S. win the gold medal in 1984, the trip to Japan, putting on the USA uniform and the social setting. Volleyball is like a little small community. I picked all that up throughout my teenage years, and just wanted to keep going. I felt so at ease with volleyball. Sometimes with basketball, even though I love it still to this day, it always felt a little more fake. With all the AAU teams I played on, there's not the close continuity of people because it's such a one-on-one game sometimes. Volleyball is such a consummate team sport, I just felt like everything about it was more real.

A lot of it was I wanted to play for my dad. I sat there and watched him lose 33 times in a row to Ball State. I didn't hate them as much as he does obviously, but it's a close second. I saw him come home every night and watch tape until four in the morning asking ``Why? What am I doing wrong?" I watched him come so close and finally win a co-conference title and then have cigars in the locker room and I saw how happy he was.

People ask me why I still play, and one of the reasons is my dad. I want to give him a gold medal and I want to give him everything. I wanted to give him a final four. I wanted to give him a national championship. I still try to make him proud. I don't know if it's being the first-born, in my character or whatever. The best words I ever hear besides ``I love you, Daddy," is hearing my father and mother say they are proud of me. That's the driving factor as to why I still play.

I called coach Knight that night. It's funny because I'm not even sure I talked to him. I think I talked to Joby Wright, but he said, ``You know what, Lloy, we had a feeling. Once we realized what kind of guy you are, we knew we'd have a hard time getting you away from your dad."

The only unfortunate thing about my decision was I wasn't able to really get to know Coach Knight. I have no doubt I would have been a better person for it. He's got to be in the top 10 of the most famous people I have ever met along with Tommy Lasorda, Tim Duncan, Richard Jefferson, Peyton Manning, Dennis Rodman, Curt Schilling, Marian Jones, Amber Veletta and Warren Sapp, but coach Knight for sure made the most lasting impression.

Dad and Coach Knight gained a lot of respect for each other in that short meeting they had, and sent congratulations back and forth over

most volleyball teams are made up of players who are friends and who don't go do their own things like they do in basketball. I just kind of fell in love with that.

It's also a true international sport. Unfortunately, in this country it really hasn't taken hold but everywhere else, besides soccer, volleyball is in the to two or three sports before basketball and it's part of their culture. Kids grow up and they have all these things called mini-volley. It's a big gym where they have 50 nets, and they are all about five foot high and the court is short and there are all these little kids out here hitting these soft, balloon-like balls back and forth, learning how to pass, learning how to set. You'd never see that here in America, but it's part of their culture. When kids get to a certain age, their parents are like, ``OK, we start volleyball now.'' How many people in Fort Wayne tell their kids that? They start baseball or soccer or basketball or PAL football. It's just a different mentality and part of it is economics. You don't need a lot to be a volleyball player. There's no pads or you don't need $150 Nikes. You just go out there with a ball and play.

A lot of people ask me about the beach, and the main reason I don't play there is I hate California. To be honest, if you are going to be a beach volleyball player, I think you need to live there to train with everybody else, and most tournaments are in that direction. Second of all, the money isn't enough. I get to make guaranteed money every year, and those guys aren't guaranteed anything. Maybe the top couple of guys are making $100,000 if they win every time. It's not like a team sport, if I get hurt I've got doctors, I've got massage therapists, I've got people taking care of me. If Mike Lambert, as an example, gets hurt, he has to pay out of pocket to get someone to fix him, and while he's not playing, he's not getting paid. When I'm not playing because I'm hurt, I'm still getting paid. To me it's a no-brainer unless you are so in love with the beach, like a lot of the guys are because they grew up there. I have no qualms about them wanting to make that career choice, but I didn't. I grew up in the Midwest. Could I play, and could I win? I think so. Do I want to move my entire family out there and rededicate my life to kind of a different game? No. For me it's just a lose-lose deal.

I don't watch volleyball on television. I don't know if that's because I play it because I think it's a great sport with the velocity of the ball, the explosiveness of the players, the smoothness of the movements, the technical aspects of your hands, the timing and all those kinds of things. Just because it is so difficult to play makes it amazing to watch. I also think that because the difficulty of playing it is why a lot of people don't watch. Even though you take the best athletes we've had like Jordan or Kobe, it's not like they can learn to spike in a week. It takes a long time to develop, and I think that hurts the growth of the sport here. If you don't start at a young age, by the time you are in high school you won't know how to play. By the time you are 18, if you don't have the skills to play you aren't going to and I think that's a real hindrance and one reason why we don't have a lot of numbers here.

We talk about the growth of the sport and I don't see it growing too much. I don't see the popularity rising. You can talk about pro leagues all you want, but I don't think it's going to happen. To be honest, I think by the time my son goes to college, there won't be men's volleyball. People talk about volleyball being a chick sport, and it kind of is in the aspect of most of the notoriety comes from the women's game now. You can turn on the TV on the weekend and find women's volleyball whether it's college or beach, but the men are pretty hard to find. The fact that there are 306 women's team and maybe a tenth as many men's college teams, if you look at the numbers it is a chick sport. Having said that, I would guess people who comment, and I would guess that's mostly Midwestern men with huge beer bellies and bald heads like most of my friends, have never seen a game because I've never heard someone after they have seen us play make that comment. Because we're tall and skinny and there's no contact, on the surface I agree it's a women's sport, but come in and stand in front of a Clay Stanley spike. See a guy who is 6-10, 250 pounds hitting the ball 80, 90 miles an hour. Better yet, you go out and just try to serve the ball over the net. It's not so easy.

I haven't been very good at trying to turn others onto volleyball. I just don't have that passion like my dad does. I would love to see the sport grow. It's been part of my life for a long time, but I just see it as a losing battle, and I'm not one of those guys who keeps bailing the boat when there's a big hole in the bottom. If someone comes along and gives us a new boat, then… maybe that's fair-weather, and if it is I'm sorry, but then I'd be happy to help. Unless I see something that is going to help promote the sport and gain momentum for the sport... you've had the same people trying for 20 years and it's not happening. I guess at some point the passion stats to fizzle without the tangible goods.

If I was starting out today, I'd call Arnie Ball. There are some programs out there... Jay Golsteyn has a boys program in Nashville, and in Indianapolis there's one, but I'm not sure there's even one in Fort Wayne right now. You'd have to find someone like my dad, find someone who is passionate about the game. If they don't know of a place to play, make them start one for you. Without dad starting a team, I wouldn't have played at all.

Volleyball is special partly because it takes that effort. If your son or daughter comes to you and says, ``I want to play volleyball" it's going to take a commitment by the mom and dad as well as the kid. I remember when we had a team in Fort Wayne when I was in junior high, we'd have kids who would drive three hours one way from Chicago for an hour-long practice and then go back. That's not only unbelievable by the kid that they'd want to do that, but also by the parents because it would easier to say, ``No, just play basketball. There's a team right down the street." It takes some sacrifice, and I think that's why there's that bond. People feel important and special in the world of volleyball because of the commitment it takes.

CHAPTER 8

I was pretty nervous starting my freshman year in college because, believe it or not, I had never really been part of a real, organized volleyball team before. From the top you have to go to these classes that are real hard, and for the first time ever I'm not living at home, I'm living with a guy who doesn't even speak English in Raul Papaleo who is from Puerto Rico and another guy I don't even know in Kevin Beck. It was a big thing, and I think I was like a typical freshman with the deer in the headlights look.

The first day of volleyball practice at IPFW, I showed up a week late because I was playing with the United States B team in Argentina. School started the last week of August, and because of that I showed up in September. There had already been a party at my apartment, and I hadn't even been there, and everyone's talking about me.

For my first official practice I show up with frosted tip hair and a goatee. So I walk into the gym, and I can't even get to the court before Dad screams, ``Tony, Fred, take that prima donna freshman downstairs and get that crap off his face!'' I, of course, have changed the word to crap from what he actually used.

I'm like ``What?''

These two grab me, one on each arm, and basically drag me. I've known Tony Luhning and Fred Malcolm, who are seniors, for a long time so I'm not afraid of getting bodily injured, but I'm like, ``This is a joke, right?'' They take me downstairs and here comes the Bic, no cream, dry shave right off my face. I humbly crawl back up to practice with this red ring around my face where my goatee used to be.

I'm thinking, ``Man, I may have made a huge mistake at that press conference.''

I don't ever remember there being a clear rule on facial hair, and I'm not even sure it was ever in existence. I got the dry shave and then slowly over time you could do whatever you wanted with your hair. I almost think it was a special one-day rule for the 6-8 kid from Woodburn maybe.

Looking back, it was just Dad. He wasn't upset about the goatee, but he knew he had to set the precedent from Day 1. He had guys like Tony and Fred who were respected and at that time were second-team all-Americans, and he was not going to get bent over backwards by his son, the so-called new king of volleyball or whatever. He was making a point.

I think I was pretty good for the most part about understanding that. Occasionally, I'd give him a push here and there to see if he'd still crack the whip at me, but I didn't give him too many hard times.

I think what was real helpful was that summer before I had worked with Tony and Fred building swimming pools, a 6 a.m. to 3 p.m., back-breaking job digging. It was just a terrible, terrible job that I loved because I love hard work and being outside. Plus, I got to pick Tony and Fred's brains about everything. We'd do that and then they'd make us go to the gym and lift weights or go play sand volleyball. I came in as a freshman much better off having spent time with them.

We were friends, yet I respected them so much that I would never question them whenever we played. If Fred said, ``This is what we should do,'' then that's what I did. I was not a leader as a freshman, I was a follower, so whatever Tony, Fred, Tom Juhnke said, that's what I tried to do. I think that was real beneficial later after those guys left as far as my becoming a leader. To be honest, Tony and Fred were not the most gifted volleyball players in the world. Fred had a nice arm, Tony was a smart guy, but he played hard and got to every ball. You take more stuff away from people like that than people who are naturally gifted. I learned so much from them about work ethic and what it was going to take to try to lead this team after they left.

My freshman year was the best year of the four. It wasn't the best team, but it was the best year because it was almost exactly like we wanted it. I was just kind of along for the ride that year, and that's part of why it was so great. There was some pressure on me, but not really like what was there the next three years when it was my show.

I really didn't feel like I was being judged by the team or by people in town. I really didn't feel any pressure that first year. It goes back to the reason I picked volleyball. I've always felt real comfortable with it and with my skills and my ability to play. I had no expectations for my own play, other than I wanted to help Dad and the team achieve these certain goals. It just seemed like a normal fit, and the pressure was much worse later.

I think Tony and Fred did a good job of keeping the expectations away from us. Dad was smart in that he never let me do any interviews, or who knows what I would have said. Tony and Fred just kept us working and kept us going. I really just got to be a role player, believe it or not. That's why I didn't feel any pressure all the way through, even at the final four, because I just did what they told me to do.

I pretty much hated Ball State since I was 12 years old, maybe even earlier. My dad lost 33 times in a row to that school, and he trained a lot of those players coaching at Harding High School. Then you go down and you know the ref is going to cheat you for five or six calls a match. For my dad, there was also the fact that he played for Don Shondell and could never get over the hump of beating his mentor kind of thing. Just seeing him come home after every loss and being so distraught, whether they lost 3-0 or 3-2 that they could have won, he'd just stay up all night watching it over and over again. The next day at church he wouldn't say a word. We felt that. I remember screaming at Chris Cooper or Chris Beerman, Randy Litchfield, Corky Robertson. I hated them. I still don't like them even though I shouldn't have anything against them. It was just the rivalry, kind of like Indiana and Purdue in basketball. That was our rivalry.

At the end of the season, we beat Ball State at Ball State to finally win the conference title and go to our first final four. I still remember that night the ball going through Stephan Stamato's hands and landing right in front of Dave Bayer to win it. I still watch that tape sometimes and watch myself immediately running over to my mom in the crowd to get a hug. All these great former players like Loren Gebert and Jay Golsteyn are sitting right there so we could share it with them.

After Dad and I found each other in the middle of the celebration, it was just a hug, and ``This is for you."

It seems like every time my Dad and I have an emotional encounter, it's pretty short sentences. ``I want to play for you," or ``This is for you," or he'd come to me at certain times in my career and say, ``Just play hard." We never used a whole lot of words to get the point across, probably because I'm sure Grandpa Ball wasn't real wordy, either, with my father.

I remember Dad was always real strict on the bus rides to and from matches, but I remember that bus ride home, Muncie to Fort Wayne, with Dad driving the van with me, Tony and Fred in the back. I won't go into too many details, but that was the best hour-long bus trip in the history of IPFW volleyball. Back then it wasn't one of those chartered busses, it was an Econoline van. Half the guys didn't have shoes on because they were so happy they forgot them at the gym. I think Tony had his Speedo on and some of the guys hadn't even showered. We were singing, ``Hawaii, here we come" and this and that. Oh, my goodness, Dad was singing, and he's never happy while driving. Best hour bus ride ever.

Getting to the NCAA Tournament finally was such a relief for Dad and the program. If you look back it was really the beginning of something – I don't credit myself for this, it was just the team and the right timing – of vaulting Dad to where he is now, one of the top coaches in the country. I really believe it changed the way my dad coaches. It gave him even more confidence. From that moment on he was even more focused than before.

We went to Hawaii for our first trip to the final four. There were two groups on that team, one who really thought we could win and one who was really just happy to go to Hawaii. I think that's why we didn't play near as well as we could have. I was real happy with my performance, and Fred played real well. In the third-place match, our team played real well against Penn State, but it didn't really matter.

I remember assistant coach Denny Johnson telling me before the USC match that this was my shot to show if I'm as good as the Freshman of the Year talk that was going on. I just remember I was going to be real aggressive and serve real aggressive and dump whenever possible because these guys had never seen a 6-8 setter play. You have Jason Stimfig and Dan Greenbaum who were 6-2, 6-3. They had never seen 6-8. I just remember I was real aggressive and I thought I had something to prove. Part of that was tipping balls to the back row to catch their defenders cheating in. I must have hit seven or eight of those. Because we were in Hawaii, we started calling them ``Pineapples."

I still remember all six players who played for that USC team. They won it the year before and they were supposed to do it again, guys like Bryan Ivie, Kevin Perkins, Dan Greenbaum, Jen Ki Lui. I'm not sure I deserved to be on the same court, especially as a freshman. Ironically, I played with some of them on the national team later. Just seeing USC, that's the powerhouse of volleyball. Everybody talks about UCLA, but USC was right up there as well. They had some of the best volleyball players ever, and for IPFW to be on the same court with them with that blasted Trojan song going off all the time... It was kind of like my David and Goliath thing.

Unfortunately, my team didn't play so well, and they beat us in four games, but I was happy with my performance. I think that performance sewed up Freshman of the Year for me.

That was my first taste of real collegiate volleyball, final four stuff.

CHAPTER 9

We knew we had a lot of guys coming back the next season, obviously not our leaders, but we still had a real good team. Dad added few guys. Neil Day showed up and he was nice, and Quinten Spiegel showed up and he was a nice role player. We just had a couple of nice pieces fall in, along with the guys we had sticking around. We felt real good about playing Ball State again for the title.

The second year was our best team out of my four years. I think we won 13 in a row, beat USC at home, and then went out and beat them at their place, beat Penn State. We started to do some things that IPFW hadn't done before. We were really playing good volleyball when we arrived at Ohio State for the conference tournament, playing with no fear. It was 3-0 in an hour and thanks for coming out. Tom Juhnke was like 15 for 16. Norman Almodovar was unbelievable. We were just a better team than everybody that year, and we knew it.

I think that's why we felt so good going into the final four that year which was at Ball State. We had our crowd and we had played there lots of times. That was the best collegiate crowd I've been a part of. I think University Arena was brand new, and you had Ball State guys cheering for us so you know something is going on, and that was probably the only time we ever got good calls at Ball State. Plus it was packed with Fort Wayne people coming down. It was an overall good volleyball experience, and it was just a great match, but unfortunately it didn't work out.

We knew Stanford was real good and was rated No. 1 coming into the semis. We were down 0-2, but guys really weren't that panicky so we just kept plugging along and came back and gained the momentum. Even to this day I would have bet money we were going to win that fifth set, but we had a crucial hitting error, and they made one great defensive play so it was 15-12 Stanford instead of us winning.

I wasn't crushed but I was disappointed. I truly believed I was going to win a title in my four years. I just believed that. Even the next year when we didn't go to the tournament, I was still confident that my final year would be it. We were hosting the final four and I had all the faith that we were going to win that. It just felt like destiny so far had played a part, so why not finish the deal?

My junior year we ran into Ohio State and future Olympic teammate Tom Hoff hitting balls out of the middle at the conference tournament. We had a great team and we killed Ball State in the semis and just ran into a team that did something we weren't used to seeing. They just kind of set behind the middle and Hoff and the other guys just hit it around.

Part of that year, though, our chemistry slowly started to come apart. We had some younger guys who were coming in who were good athletes but not necessarily good volleyball players. The burden shifted on Norman and me as far as trying to be leaders and we were never really comfortable with that. Some of the Puerto Rican players started thinking about getting married instead of playing volleyball, and we slowly kind of grew apart. We were still friends but it wasn't like before.

Some of us reacted well to what happened, and some of us didn't. That was when I started having some troubles with the national team, the summer I got cut from the World University Games team and I started to question some of my own playing stuff. Luckily I hooked into Rick Butler that summer and he basically told me I was too overweight, drinking too much beer and I wasn't concentrating enough. He said basically, either you're going to get yourself together and make it or you're going to fall apart like lot of people do and not make it. It was a wake-up call for me and I came back for my senior year fit and ready. Some guys didn't.

CHAPTER 10

Toward the end of my junior year, I got arrested. The ironic part was that it was reported in the paper that I was out celebrating my 21st birthday, but this actually happened two weeks after my birthday. My birthday was February 17 and this was March 1 or so because on my birthday I had the flu. My family and I went to Chi Chi's for dinner, but I was dying and didn't even have a drink on my 21st birthday because I was so sick.

Two weeks later I was feeling better and it was a Tuesday night which is a big night at O'Sullivans, this local bar that's pretty popular in Fort Wayne. I'm living downtown then, literally four minutes from the bar, and for some reason I had driven down there, maybe thinking someone would drive. The whole team is there and everyone is buying me shots, this and that, and come around 1 a.m. I'm tired and said I'm going to go home.

I don't really remember anyone saying don't drive or this or that. I just remember walking out and getting into my white Ranger and driving down the road. I swear to this day I'm not sure I did anything to warrant being pulled over. People told me someone from the bar reported me to the police. True or not, I don't know. I do know I wasn't even out of third gear in the truck when I got pulled over, and you could still see O'Sullivan's in my rear view mirror. Somebody told me the arresting officer called one of the radio stations the next morning and bragged, ``Guess who I pulled over."

The breathalyzer – the limit was .10 then – I was .11, and they take me downtown and book me. I spend the night in jail with about 30 other people because they are bringing in guys from bar fights, some of whom are bloody.

I sobered up in a real hurry. There was a big African-American guy, he must have weighed 320 pounds, there named Tony, and I befriended him in a hurry. As soon as I walked in, he's like ``You're tall,'' and I'm just trying to make some dialogue because he was the scariest guy in there. Luckily, he had a great personality. He said he had been at a place called ``The Boom Boom Room,'' which I had never heard of and probably never want to. It was the same thing, the cops got him for drinking and driving. He was the nicest, biggest guy you've ever met, so I sat next to him all night and made sure he was my buddy, in a good way.

As this is going on, I feel real sober real quick. I had never even been called down to the principal's office before. The whole time this is going on, I'm thinking about my dad. They're like, ``Do you want to call somebody?'' but I keep saying, ``No, I'll just sit here and take it.''

I'm not going to say it was a good lesson because I'm not sure if I learned anything from it or not except don't drink and drive. Let's just say I'm not planning on going back to jail.

Then that next day… I hadn't called my mom and dad from jail. I just wouldn't. It wasn't that I was afraid, but that's not a phone call I could make to my parents at 3 a.m. So I waited until the next day, and they let me go on my own recognizance. A teammate picked me up and we go directly to Dad's office, and I say, ``I got arrested last night.''

I will remember that look probably for the rest of my life. It was as the first point and time in my life that I knew my dad was disappointed in me. I wasn't afraid to tell him. I was afraid to tell my mom, but I wasn't afraid to tell my dad. Just the look of disappointment on his face, I knew would be devastating.

I go to practice that afternoon and I sit down in front of the whole team and tell them what happened. The chancellor decided that because it wasn't at a team function or at the school, legally he couldn't do anything to me for the next game against Ball State. My dad said, ``If you guys want me to sit Lloy out of the next match as punishment, I'll sit him out.'' They all say no.

Practices were – let's just say I probably lost 10 pounds over those next four days from getting worked over. I probably didn't say more than 10 words in any of those practices. I just took the beating.

I'm also taking a beating in the media because the cops called the media. Most of the media would not report misdemeanors, but they reported this. I found it somewhat ironic that it got reported, but the gist of it was I was in the wrong. I'm not going to complain about it. It sure made a lot of good fodder for the Ball State fans when they came up that Friday.

So we play Ball State, we won and I sprained my ankle on the last play. We killed them 3-0, but the tough part was still coming. I had not told my mom about this but that day it was in the paper, and she found out because someone at work gave it to her. Real nice. I had not talked to her before the game, but I keep looking up into the stands and I can just see in her face that she knows. I don't even know how we won because I wasn't thinking about the game, I was thinking about this confrontation with my mom that was coming.

Luckily, I sprained my ankle so they took me right downstairs and put me in a whirlpool in the training room. It wasn't more than 10 minutes later that my dad comes in and tells everybody else to clear out. Then in walks my mom. As soon as she walked in, I just started crying and I just said, ``I'm so sorry. I'm sorry it got out that way and I'm sorry I didn't have enough guts to tell you about it. I'm sorry that it happened." She's crying, and like my Mom always does, she says, ``I love you," and gives me a big hug. It was all going to be all right, and I knew it would be, but I was just afraid to tell her.

I had to do a lot of community service after that. I had the court thing, too, but I probably went to an elementary school every week, not talking about drinking and driving but talking about making good choices. Most of the kids knew what happened to me.

I had six months of probation with no license, and six months of alcohol and drug school twice a week. I couldn't have any alcohol in my system and there was urine testing every time I went. Then I had

50 hours of community service. It all cost about $1,400 because I had to take a loan out to pay for it.

Anybody who knows me knows I like to drink. Am I a hard drinker? No, but I am the epitome of a social drinker. I love to have beers and cocktails and talk about everything with everybody. I like karaoke, I like singing, and I like dancing. I love wedding receptions. I love to have a good time, and if that involves a six pack, then so be it. I just now understand the responsibility that comes along with that good time.

CHAPTER 11

We had another good year when I was a senior. That's the year we played UCLA at home to start the season and we played pretty well even though we didn't win. But I could kind of feel it slipping away from us because the focus was gone. I knew I was about done and I started thinking about the national team way too soon. We had a good season but showed up at the conference tournament not ready. I think we just thought everyone would just lay down for us, and Ball State had obviously decided 15 losses in a row was just darn enough. They played great, and we panicked. I didn't play well. It was just a meltdown.

Then things got really weird. IPFW Assistant Athletic Director Dan Gebhart wrote the NCAA Men's Volleyball Committee petitioning to get IPFW the at-large bid to the tournament which we were hosting. We had crushed Stanford during the regular season and they would have been the No. 2 team to come off the West Coast.

I honestly never thought we'd get it even with what Dan was trying. To be brutally honest, part of me wishes we had not gotten it. If we had won after that, it would have been tainted in everybody's eyes in volleyball except our own in this area. It's at IPFW, and there are already two Midwest/East Coast teams so Southern California is going to be ticked off. I'm not even sure it was right. By the criteria it was, but were we better than Stanford? In the long run it actually hurt my Dad's program because they wouldn't come out here to play them.

It was a second chance, but it was double the pressure because now we have to play well. Unfortunately, the bad thing about college athletes is we don't bounce back real well. On a pro team, I've learned now that if you spanked me last night, I can come back tonight and get you. In college, we never recovered from that Ball State loss. Even if I had not hurt myself, we would not have won in that final four. We lost it that night at home against Ball State in the conference tournament.

So after we lost to Ball State, we had about four days of school and partying because we have a week left before school's out and I'm not going to see these guys any more. We were hitting it pretty good and we weren't practicing.

All of a sudden we get the call that we're in the tournament, and I haven't done a thing for four days. That's the whole reason when we found out I tried to go work out, tried to do stuff, which, of course, it was the wrong thing to do. I knew I needed to get a workout in so I called some of my buddies and say let's go run some hoops and get some exercise. We go down to a local place we know that has open gym, and 10 minutes in, boom. I was in the low post and a guy throws the ball in. Another guy reaches over my back to knock the ball away and instead hits my hand so my hand ends up going straight at the ball which hits my index finger straight on and it pops out to the side. It hurt, but I figured it was just jammed. I'm kind of pulling on it trying to get it back in. It's starting to get fat, so OK, I'm out. I go back and ice it all night, but I know something is wrong because just touching it sends me through the roof.

The next day I go to practice and we're all excited because we've got practice, we've got a second chance and we can get ready for the final four. I'm getting it taped up and the first ball I try to bump, it's like somebody took a hammer and just hit me with it. So I go to Dad and say, ``Something is wrong.''

``What are you talking about?''

``I hurt my finger.''

So they send me over to Redi-med and sure enough, it's broken in half.

I hadn't told Dad how I did it yet so he still thinks I did in volleyball. After we get the x-ray and get the surgery lined up, I tell him what happened. He didn't swear, he didn't say anything. He just gave me the headshake again. In jest, he says things to people about being upset, but I don't think he was because I had played basketball all four years every Sunday in the Hicksville, Ohio, League. Two years we were the champs. Basketball is part of my thing, and I love to play.

If you look back, you can say I was so stupid or this and that. Yeah, I make very good money playing volleyball, but I still go the YMCA and play every Thursday. Is that smart? For some people who don't do what I do? No. For me, it's how I recharge my batteries and get a great workout in. I try to be careful, but by the same token I could fall off my deck. Injuries happen, and this was part of my routine.

I had the surgery on the Tuesday before we played on Friday night. Dr. Christopher LaSalle put two pins in my left index finger that are still there today. The bone didn't break horizontally, it was in a straight line along the finger. They had to put the two pins in from the inside out to kind of squeeze those bones back together again. The doctor said, ``You can play, it won't re-break but it's gonna hurt." That's when we tried to practice with me playing opposite. I had a big plastic splint on there because you can't wear metal during a match so I couldn't really block, but I could hit. We found out pretty quickly in that match that wasn't going to get it done though.

UCLA was pounding us so I start setting in the third set and we still lose. It was like having a cucumber for a finger. I left the tape on that was underneath the padding. I don't remember what it felt like because at that time I was so angry with myself and so frustrated from us being down 0-2 and just the situation I had put myself and my team in. I don't remember feeling much of anything except being upset and having the worst feeling you can possibly have at the end.

I was real sad my career was over. I spent that night with a few friends from outside the volleyball circle and broke down a little bit. It had been four great years of achieving a lot, but yet not achieving what I wanted. Socially, it was four great years, academically it wasn't too bad except for that last semester. I always stayed eligible and did what I had to do to make sure I could play. I don't lie to people and tell them I was there for an education because I wasn't. I was there to play volleyball and I got my education afterward.

It was the greatest four years of my life. I saw my dad every day, my mom got to see every home match I ever played. My grandparents saw me play every game. It was sad that I knew it was over. I was excited because I knew in a week I was leaving for the national team, but I was a little scared about that because Fort Wayne was home, and I just felt so comfortable for those four years. I was leaving for San Diego and I was nervous and scared and all those things.

But for that one night I was a little inconsolable.

CHAPTER 12

About a month before the conference tournament my senior year, I got my first tattoo on a trip to State College, Pennsylvania, just because I always wanted one. That was kind of like my transition phase. About three months before the final four, I broke up with Sarah, whom I had been dating for about two-and-a-half years by then. I shaved my head. I went, not crazy, but I knew the end was close and I knew I wasn't going to graduate yet, so I kind of blew off school a little bit. I knew I was going to the national team.

So I got a tattoo. It was after the Friday night match. A friend of mine, Salima Davidson, who set for Penn State, called the tattoo guy to see if he would stay later. We went late that night around 10, and had a couple beers and got my first tattoo. There was kind of a party and there were maybe 20 people there. The guy made me real nervous because I think he had been drinking a while. I was like, I don't want some drunk guy tattooing me, but as soon as he started tattooing, he was pretty focused and it turned out all right.

It's an ankh, an Egyptian cross. All the other ones have some kind of significance in my life, but that one really doesn't, to be honest. I just wanted a tattoo.

I put a bandage on it and didn't let anybody know about it the next night before the match, and I still think I dove a couple times. Luckily, it wasn't too big so it didn't cause too much pain.

Dad just rolled his eyes and said, whatever. Mom said, ``You're such a beautiful boy, why would you do that to your body? It doesn't make any sense to me." Then she pulled the Grandma Bert card, her mother.

``Grandma Bert would be so disappointed in you." Mom always tried to throw some reality in.

I hadn't gotten one to that point because of fear of my parents. I had gotten earrings in college, and that was kind of my first rebellion against my parents. I was a really, really good kid, probably too good, and that's maybe why I didn't have too many friends in high school. I didn't drink, I really didn't swear a whole lot and went to church every Sunday. Once I got to college, I let loose a little bit like I suppose everyone does. I drank a little bit, I got an earring. My Dad was not real excited about that so I didn't ever wear it around him, and of course not in practice. My dad as a coach tried to keep being my father and coaching as two separate things.

After the first one, my fascination with tattoos kind of progressed. I don't know if you've ever watched tattoo shows on TV, but it is addictive, from the experience in the shop with some tatted up guy or girl doing it to you, to the pain that it is, to knowing it's there forever, all that stuff. It's hard to stop. Every year I want to get another one, but luckily I've controlled myself to where only at significant times in my life do I now get one.

I started with the ankh. As Sarah and I became more serious, I put her initials above it. When I knew we were together for sure, I had that put on after we had moved together to California.

Then IPFW basketball player Sean Gibson and I all got tattoos of a triangle with a skeleton inside, his with a basketball and mine with a volleyball inside. It's on my left calf. It kind of means sports forever, triangle of three friends and you're 19 so we thought that was significant. It was a good time when we had it done. I met Sean my senior year in high school which was his freshman year at IPFW. I came in to shoot hoops at IPFW and he was playing basketball so we started playing one-on-one and kind of hit it off. That next year he said, well, let's live together, and at that time it was kind of taboo for athletes from different sports to do that. Later we went down to New Albany where he lived and met his folks and had a great time. The second year, his brother Shane transferred up and he came to live with us. After that, those two guys were like my brothers. So that's why I got that tattoo.

Once I moved out to California, that's when I really started to get into it with the good artists, world-renowned tattoo people. That's when I got the ``Anger is a Gift" tattoo on my right shoulder. It's words from a song by Rage Against the Machine. The picture is, unfortunately for my mother, a devil, but it has no religious meaning whatsoever. Those first couple of years with the national team I was playing and partying pretty hard, and when I played, everyone thought I was so angry all the time and I was mad because I was shouting at my own team and at the other team. Unfortunately I was out of control a little bit, but that tattoo symbolizes the mood I was in when I was playing at that time.

Then, once I got that figured out and started to relax a little bit, I got a snake with a volleyball on the left arm. There was like a year, year and a half in there when I had moved to California, and I had broken up with Sarah, that tattoos started coming, I was making my own money playing volleyball, I was the new kid on the block thinking I'm hot stuff. I was just doing stuff that's not really Lloy Ball-type stuff. Eventually, I got the reality check that I wasn't playing very well, I'm not the starting setter, and Dad is like, ``What are you doing?" I finally just woke up and started to figure it out and everything started to come full circle, like the snake. All those things that the snake represents kind of came around and at the end it was volleyball that kind of held my life together. It still does to this day. It's always the calming factor. If my kid doesn't sleep that night, or I didn't get paid my contract money, whatever it is, if I go out and play on the court, I don't think about any of that other stuff.

On the tattoo, the volleyball is blocking the snake from connecting and taking control. The snake is squeezing, but the volleyball just stays the same because in the end volleyball was the thing that kept me going. When I thought I was going to get in trouble, I'd think about volleyball and say, ``Maybe not a good choice." Volleyball was always there as a crutch. To this day, I know I don't do some things because of what volleyball means to me.

Then right before my first Olympics I got San Luis Ray in Scandinavian runes etched on the inside of my right bicep. I got that with Ethan Watts who was also on the 1996 Olympic team because it was the street we lived on with six other guys, all of us trying out for the team.

Ethan and I both got that to remember that little house we all had to live in because we couldn't afford anything more. He and I were the only ones to go to the Olympics.

Of course I got the Olympic rings on my back after I had made the roster, right between my shoulder blades. I waited until right before we left, even though they announced the team something like two months prior. If I had gotten it done right then, I still had two months to get hurt, and if I don't go to the Olympics but I have the Olympic rings, I'd kind of look like an idiot so that's why I waited. That's probably still my favorite after that tattoos for my kids.

In 2000 I got a big USA on my lower back inside a star with the pattern of an American flag in the background. I felt like I was going to be a two-time Olympian and I just wanted to do it again. That one took the longest to get and was the most painful. It took two-and-a-half hours of being bent over, sitting in a chair with my hands almost on the ground because your skin had to be stretched tight. Otherwise, if you did it sitting normally, then it would be all out of sorts when you stretched.

I was bent over and my legs fell asleep about an hour in. Second of all, the tattoo parlor was not air conditioned, and it was about 95 degrees that day so there was literally a pool of sweat underneath me. Luckily, Sarah was there to talk to and they rolled a TV in front of me so I could watch a baseball game that was going on. It's also right on my spine which is one of the most painful places. I lost interest about an hour and a half in and thought, ``This was a really bad idea," but after it was done, it's one of my favorites.

Then I've got tattoos for my kids, Dyer on my right arm and Mya with a little princess on my left shoulder. My son could care less and doesn't even see the tattoos. When I got the new one for his baby sister, I pointed it out to him and he just kept on walking.

The only thing about tattoos I regret is that in 1996, I bought into the promos and stuff they ran on me before the Olympics and started believing in them a little bit. That was a situation where I sure wish I had had my dad closer to me or someone at the time to kind of slap me a little bit. I blame myself for the overexposure and the stupidity that went with some of the publicity and stuff. I didn't know any better. I was 24, and in the ``Anger is a Gift" stage. Even though I listen to that music, anybody who knows me knows that's not me. When I play, I'm emotional but there's nothing real angry about how I play.

I just kind of let them feed me this and I went with it because I got some attention, and I was going to be in magazines. If we had won the gold medal, it probably would not have ended real well as far as going down this kind of path that was really not me. It really detracted from the way I played, to be honest, and I was so caught up in this little media thing we had going that sometimes I forgot why I was there. It was just a promotional thing, but in a team sport it really hurts the team when someone starts thinking they are above the rest, and I did. I admit it. The tattoos became a person my family and friends knew I wasn't, and unfortunately it took me struggling in Atlanta and some other things to realize I just needed to be myself. I don't think I'm a rebel at all. I like to have a good time and unfortunately tattoos come with a stigma of rebelling and being out of control, and anybody who watches me play knows I'm not that.

I don't know if I'm done getting them, though. I'd like to get one more, kind of a big one on my back. Sarah is trying to draw something up for it, bringing together the three titles I've won. No American has won the titles in Greece, Italy and Russia like I have so I'd like to have something to tie that all together. Then I'll probably be done. In a couple of more years I might be all wrinkly and fat so they may not look good anyway.

Once my son turns 18, if he wants a tattoo, he can do what he wants. If he wants an earring he can have one. Hopefully, by that time, I've instilled in him what my parents instilled in me: Tattoos don't make the man.

Sarah loves them, but she doesn't have any. She hates blood and pain but she likes it when it's inflicted on me.

But I still like tattoos because I think they are cool, and my wife thinks they are sexy. What else do you need?

CHAPTER 13

Before I broke my finger, I really thought I was ready to go to the national team in 1994. I had a great senior year and we should have gotten to the final four on our own had we not choked in the final against Ball State. And even though we lost to Ball State, had I been healthy, I think we would have given UCLA much more of a run than we did. They were ready to be beaten, because obviously they were in the next match by Penn State.

I went out and joined the national team right away and I still had a splint on my hand so I was a little nervous about that, but right from Day 1 I felt at ease. I think that goes back to from 17 years of age on always having some kind of USA jersey hanging up somewhere in the closet. It just felt right, and I think it helped when I got there.

There were some veterans like Bob Ctvrtlik, Eric Sato and Scott Fortune, but there were also some guys I had played against in college like Bryan Ivie, Brett Hilliard, Dan Greenbaum, Jason Stimfig. I always thought Greenbaum was a great setter, obviously having won a national championship at USC, but I always felt that I was as good as he was. Then being comfortable with that and then coming in and performing so well, so quickly, kind of fed my confidence, and the skills that I was still improving on. I was by far a better server, blocker and defensive player than I was an actual setter. Setting was probably the last thing I got real good at, oddly enough.

I was working so hard and training so hard because I finally had gotten to start living the dream I always thought I would get to live.

Part of my early success was because of my height. Besides Peter Blange who at 6-9 was a 1996 gold medalist from Holland, there was no one as tall as I was as a setter. To be honest, in hindsight, I'm not sure it was a big deal, but it's just another thing people like to talk about reinventing the game. Doug Beal reinvented it with the two-passer system and then Carl McGown with the read blocking system, and the big setter was just a reinvention of that position. You still had to set the ball because it doesn't do you any good to have a big guy who can't set. I do think especially in a time when I started playing, offenses were much slower, there were a lot more high balls going to the left side than there are now, so having a big guy out there to block was an advantage.

In my first big tournament, the World Championships in 1994, we won a bronze medal. It's the only medal I've won in a major competition with the U.S., and it's because we blocked a lot of balls out there, not because I was a great setter. Obviously, offensively we've never had a guy, except maybe for Javier Gaspar, who dumped the ball as much as I did, and I had a real good jump serve. It became kind of like having an opposite in the setting position and it just added another offensive weapon to the team. I think it did change the game for a little bit, but I think it has changed back a little bit now. They are going back to smaller guys who can run faster offenses. There's just not as much left-side attacking as there used to be with all the pipes and quick hitters and guys flying all over the place, so having a big goofball like me out there really doesn't give you that much of an advantage. I'd like to think Peter and I helped change the game at least for a little while.

Right out of the gate I had a great experience out in San Diego when I joined the national team. Within seven weeks, I had the starting job. Here you go, a guy who is not even a year out of college, it's a world championships year and I get to take my first trip to Athens as the starting setter. I remember calling Dad every night because I was so nervous. In our group we had Argentina, Brazil and Cuba, I think. Sure enough we go undefeated in the pool play somehow. We get a nice crossover quarter match against Korea that we win 3-0. Dad asked me if we were playing well, and I said, ``I don't know, but we just keep winning. I'm just doing whatever the heck they tell me to, but I'm not sure what I'm doing."

In the semis we play Holland and we lose in five, 15-13 in the fifth game so we have to play Cuba for the bronze medal. I'll always remember that because we were so disappointed. I was excited about the whole thing and the chance to win a medal, but guys who had been there a while and had won stuff already were disappointed and we have to turn around the next day and play a real good Cuba team. I remember Ctvrtlik stood up after coach Sturm was done, and said, ``Wait a minute. Do not take this lightly. This may be the only chance in your career you have to win a medal." Sure enough, we went out and just banged them down. We got to be on the platform with Italy and Holland, and it's still the biggest achievement with the national team that I've ever had.

I've been the starting setter ever since. Three World Cups, three World Championships, four Olympics, five World Leagues – there aren't any bigger tournaments than those, and I played in all of them at least three times. It would obviously be nice to be able to throw in three gold medals, but that hasn't happened yet.

CHAPTER 14

The first time I recall watching the Olympics was in 1984, sitting with my dad watching Dusty Dvorak and the boys win the gold medal. I remember saying, ``That's something I want to do.'' Then of course in 1988, we watched Scott Fortune hit that last overpass down to clinch the gold medal and I was like, ``Shoot, I have to get on that team because they just win all the time. That looks easy.'' Then I remember watching in 1992 with Bob Samuelson getting the red card and the whole team shaving their heads in support, coming all the way back and winning a bronze medal.

We followed the Olympics pretty seriously, but 1984 was the first one where I was really amazed. I had seen volleyball at the high school level when dad was coaching and he had started the IPFW program by then, but this was a whole different sport. These guys were flying and hitting the ball hard. It was kind of like watching the sport as its purest form. Back then volleyball was a lot purer sport. It was kind of like watching the old Boston Celtics play basketball – pass, pass, pass for the lay-up. That's the way volleyball was back then and I just kind of fell in love with the rhythm of it.

So I hoped my Olympics experience in 1996 would be similar to that. I was 24 years old, but unfortunately I was just too immature. Maybe Jeff Stork would have been a better choice as the setter. The team had been playing well with me up to that point so the thought was there was no need to change, but the Olympics are a different deal. I lost concentration pretty much from the get-go. You walk into the stadium for the opening ceremonies and there are over 100,000 Americans and it felt like they were basically just clapping for me. You have the USA uniform on, you march in with all the USA people, but it's really like they are clapping for you. It was the most hair-raising experience that I've had in my international career. I always tell people that all Olympics are different, but that first one, you're just like a kid in the candy store. It's so overwhelming. I mean the hair on my arms probably never laid down for two weeks.

Despite that, we came out and started to play real well. We whipped Argentina 3-0. We hosed down Poland 3-0, and we're cruising along. People are like, ``One more match and we're on to the quarterfinals,'' and that's part of the problem. We thought we had it in, but we played Brazil the next night and we get smacked 0-3. I start saying some things I shouldn't say about the coaches and the team because I got yanked, and should have gotten yanked because I was terrible, but at the time I thought I was so good that I probably shouldn't have been taken out. Anyway, it just started falling apart.

The next match we bounced back well with Cuba, 13-13 and I'll never forget it. I set Ivie a D with no block and a little defensive sub named Ricardo Vantes came in to play the left back and they left him alone. Ivie buries it and he digs it straight up and they go to Joel Despaigne left side for the point. Now it's 13-14 in the fifth set. We call time out and Rod Wilde is like, ``Well, that was a good play, the guy just dug it.'' I was like, ``Well, I'm going to run it again because I think Cuba will do the exact same thing as last time.'' We get a great pass and run double quicks and they both jump with them so there's a big hole and I set Ivie a back row ball. He hits it hard and clips the antenna and we lose. It's not that it's his fault because we had chances throughout the whole match. That was really demoralizing because if we win that match, we're in the quarterfinals. We came back the following night and played Bulgaria which wasn't very good, but we didn't play well and lost in five games. It was more mental than anything, but we're out and we're done.

The biggest thing I remember is Bob again. When Bob spoke it always seemed like it was coming out of a Rocky Balboa movie, something that needed to be written down almost. Obviously, he wasn't saying too much, and I ask him if he's OK. He looks at me and goes, ``I just hope the sun comes up tomorrow.'' It was almost like he wanted to cry, and I just then realized what had happened and how important it was.

Not that I blew it, but collectively we let it slip away when, if I was setting in 1996 like I am now, it never would have happened. I would have made the team get to the next round somehow, someway. At 24 you don't see it until it's over and a wiser man like Ctvrtlik pointed it out to us.

There was a lot of criticism. I didn't block well in the entire tournament. I came in as the best server on the team and I didn't serve well the whole tournament. Then you throw in the commentators complaining about me not setting enough quick offense, but we never really did that. Besides Ivie, who was jumping all the time, Nygaard wasn't a very good quick attacker. We just didn't have the make-up of the team to do that. If you're the quarterback and you throw the ball to one guy and he drops it, there's not much you can say when somebody asks why you didn't throw it to the other guy. Arm-chair quarterbacking is probably the easiest thing to do.

Because of the criticism, I was a mess for a while. Everyone heard what they were saying and I wasn't calm and cool enough or mature enough to make the responses necessary to the comments, and there was a good two or three months where I was pretty messed up. I probably took it a little too hard, but when you're 24 and you've spent the last 10 years of your life building toward that moment, it hurts when you realize it didn't quite finish how you'd have written it.

Rod called the offense all the time anyway. Back then I had zero autonomy as far as what I could select compared to what I can do now, and they did the same thing with Jeff for the most part. People have to realize the offense that Jeff or Dusty Dvorak ran in 1984 and 1988 was set up because of float serves and there were two passers. By 1996 serving was much tougher. That's why Holland won because they had three guys who could jump serve. We only had one guy. There was no doubt that Jeff was a great setter, but to try stepping into an offense that wasn't exactly the same offense he had run four or eight years before… We didn't have a Steve Timmons coming out of the back to pound everything whenever we got in trouble. He was still trying to run Xs with Bob Ctvrtlik and Xs were kind of over with by that time.

As bad as I felt after the 1996 Olympics, I wasn't as devastated as I was after the later ones. I knew I would be back, and I had a "just happy to be there" feeling most of the time. I regret that, but I was 24. I had no doubt that I would win a gold medal eventually.

Even though we didn't win, I still felt like I was on top of the world. The media was all over me, I had a good contract offer and I was getting married in a few months. Life was good. I guess I was so into my life I really didn't have time or energy to mourn the loss in Atlanta.

CHAPTER 15

It just so happened that this team from Toray, Japan, was there at the Olympics looking for a setter. Alec Peters was an assistant coach at USC who was trying to become an agent, and I really didn't have anybody because it was very hard to find anybody who knows anything about volleyball at that time. Even though I didn't play well, Alec made a heck of a pitch and got me a contract with this team. It was for two years for more money than I had ever heard about at that time, so I left for Japan about a month and a half later.

When I started in 1996, Japan was the best-paying league, not only because it had the highest dollar amount, but because you had to work half the time to get it. Japan's volleyball season was four months long, and ends in the middle of March whereas the rest of the leagues go through May. And the money was at least double in Japan. Being a younger guy and a setter, my contract was right around $200,000, but the hitters who went over there could earn around $400,000 to $450,000, which since the days of Karch Kiraly and Steve Timmons, playing in Italy was unheard of. If you can make $400,000 in four months, that's a pretty good deal.

At that time I could have stayed with the national team because they had a year-round program, and some of the guys went to the beach. I was making $3,000 a month on the national team, and this was more money than I've ever heard of. It was just so exciting.

I had always planned on playing overseas ever since I got that bug from when I was 17. I love to travel, I love hotels and I love crazy foods and I love playing in front of thousands of people who love volleyball even though I can't understand what the heck they are saying. It's probably as much as a volleyball player can feel like a rock star.

I got to take Sarah with me, so we were two kids from rural Indiana going to live in Mishima, Japan, which is right at the base of Mount Fuji, one hour by Supertrain from Tokyo.

I'd been to Japan many times with the national team, but Sarah had never been there before. It's a different world, not only because of the travel but because the Asian languages are much more difficult for us to learn. Even though we tried, it was impossible. They all have black hair, and the people are for the most part shorter than us. It's the most expensive place in the world, it's an island and you can have fish for breakfast if you choose. They have a culture based on hierarchy where if you are under this guy and he asks you to do something you do it and don't ask why. They pretty much are a country that has gotten so strong because they work harder and longer than we do. It's a place where there are a lot of closet alcoholics because of the pressure.

It's a great place. The Japanese people are very honest, up front and loyal. They are friendly in a very childish way. When the women giggle, they cover their mouths so you can't see their teeth. If someone says something that is not correct, you don't make eye contact. You take your shoes off and put flip flops on when you enter someone's house. There was a lot of green tea and chatting. It's just a nice place with nice people.

We slept on Tatami floors. They brought an American bed in for us even though it's not normal. We had a great apartment, but sleeping on the Tatami floors, that's the best sleep I've ever had. It was hard but it kind of forms to your back. It's a whole big room, so for a guy like me who rolls around a lot, I wasn't going to hit any walls or fall off.

Of the four places I've played now, it was definitely the biggest cultural difference. Even now you can find a McDonald's just about everywhere, but they have done a nice job of keeping their own heritage and culture.

My team, and I didn't know this going in, is known because it used a lot of the old school training principles. Some of the teams had already come around with the more modern training techniques, but our team, not so much. There was still some physical violence against players, especially the younger ones if they didn't perform correctly. There was a lot of yelling. The first time I saw some physical contact, I looked at my translator, and she was like ``Don't worry Lloy, that won't happen to you." I was thinking this could be over in a hurry.

If the supervisor representing the company which was our team sponsor – someone who had probably played volleyball once in his life – came in and told you to set with the back of your hands, you set with the back of your hands. If he told you to spike with two hands, you spiked with two hands. You don't ask questions, you just do it, until he leaves and then you go back to doing it the right way.

We trained six hours a day. I weighed 205 pounds when I played there. (I weigh 230 now and my normal playing weight is 225.) All you eat there is rice and fish and because we trained so hard, you can't keep weight on. They drink beer at every meal, and they are the skinniest people in the world because they train so long and so hard.

That was great for my game because that's where I really learned how to set. When you have to set 11 Japanese guys who aren't very good, the ball better be real good and right where they can hit it. After three years there, my setting improved significantly.

My translator was Takako, and funny enough, she married Takaki. I felt bad for her because Sarah and I basically used her for everything. If we needed airplane tickets or we wanted pizza at 2 a.m. we called her to order it for us. What are you going to do, call the pizza place? They answer ``konbanwa" and you're already in trouble. That mean's "Good evening" in Japanese. Whenever we'd pick up our phone, we'd say ``Moshi, Moshi" which means hello on the phone and they'd start rambling on thinking we understood Japanese.

Our coach didn't speak any English whatsoever. I'm still 24 and I'm still ripping and roaring with a lot of energy on the court, and I'd be angry sometimes, especially when you can't communicate and you have guys who hit it out of bounds with no block up, so I'd kick the ball and stuff like that. The coach had Takako make up signs because the guys didn't now how to say stuff like "higher" or "slower" or "closer." So after a while, I'd hear ``Lloy-san, Lloy-san," and I'd look over to see this big sign "Calm down." The next one would be ``Relax." Sarah would be sitting behind the bench just rolling because after a while it became just comical.

After one match we lost, I went to a separate gym and started kicking balls and saying stuff we can't put in the book, and all of the guys start walking by and looking at Sarah like, "Has he lost his mind?" She was like, ``Just leave him alone." After that was when all the calm down and relax signs started.

Japanese teams are only allowed one international player, and a lot of times they just let the foreign player do what he does. You are already making 100 times what the Japanese players are making, so you're pretty much just a hired gun. As long as he doesn't embarrass the team or the coach, everything is fine. I made sure I never got in the face of the coach or anything like that. If I did need to talk to him I did it with Takako behind closed doors. To save face is very important in Japan.

Besides losing so much weight, we had training camps when there was downtime where we had to go to some mountain retreat and basically train all morning, come home and try to sleep for an hour, eat and go back and train again. On the first night, I came out about 6 p.m. and said, ``Where's the bus?" They're like, ``No bus, Lloy-san." We're about five miles from where we're staying and all of a sudden the coach starts handing out weight vests. Coach is like, ``Home, home." We just practiced for six hours and he wants me to run home about five miles, and I know your parents always say it was uphill both ways, but this actually was uphill, and he's got a stopwatch. I'm thinking, ``What did Alec Peters get me into?"

So of course, they all take off, and I'm like, ``Whatever." At first I tried to keep up, but the other players knew what was coming and they were prepared for this. I'd have gone a little lighter in practice if I had known I was going to have to run home with a weight vest on. About 30 minutes later I finally get there and my knees are shot, my back hurts and I throw the weight vest off. We did that every day for 10 days. It was crazy.

Those three years in Japan are by far the best shape I've ever been in. I didn't actually play real well, because my body fat was down to about 6 percent, and I get tired real quick if I'm not at about 10 percent body fat. I have to have something for fuel, so I was getting tired in about an hour. I had no meat on my bones, so I was just exhausted.

But I went back for the money. I had a two-year contract the first time and then they asked me to come back for a third. Sarah and I talked about it. Even though the training was hard and the volleyball wasn't very good, it was good money for a young couple that had just gotten married. To be making six figures like that right off the get-go was setting us up in the right position and they treated us real well. Minus the heartache and being tired all the time and the volleyball not being at a real high level, it was a good situation. I got to sleep at home every night.

The volleyball was comparable to the best collegiate teams. They just aren't very big. We did have one other 6-9 guy, but most of them were 6-3, 6-4 and they weren't great jumpers. Technically, they weren't very good, and to be honest they didn't have a lot of heart. I think one of the reasons they kept wanting me back was, even though they wanted me to calm down a little bit, they also needed the drive and the emotion which some of these guys didn't have. There were a lot of mistakes. Because there was so much pressure put on them by the coaches and by the company to play well, some of the players didn't deal with it real well, and they made a lot of mistakes.

In my last year we finished second and lost in the finals. It was by far the best year they had ever had, and then just a few years after that they got a Russian hitter and won the championship. I was very happy for them.

Sarah and I walked everywhere because getting a car was impossible. Not only do they drive on the wrong side, but I can't read the signs. Anywhere we needed to go long we took the train which was great because it was fast and comfortable. Besides walking to practice about 20 minutes every day and then back, we'd walk to the grocery store. Sarah was in good shape, too. It was hilly because we were right at the base of Mount Fuji. They finally got me a bicycle my last year and I rode that around with 30 million other Japanese people.

It was a cool experience. Besides the volleyball, it was probably the best place we've lived. I stay in touch with one or two guys on every team I have played with. It is hard to make tons of friends because as a paid worker, I am there for a job, not to socialize, but there are always one or two guys and their families that we connected with.

After that first year in Japan, I knew I had the right choice with Sarah because we spent every minute of every day together. If we had practice, she went. If we had a match somewhere, she was the only woman ever on the team bus or on the team plane and we stayed together on the road. One of the reasons she went with us was that Takako was not there and if something had happened, and I'm not there, who's Sarah going to call for help. So it was mainly for her safety and her situation.

Literally, it was 24-7 together with this woman and we didn't have one argument or one problem. At the end of that season, I said, ``I'm marrying this one. Quickly.''

CHAPTER 16

Because volleyball is so big in Japan, I became something of a celebrity there but that was OK because for some reason, I've always felt comfortable in the spotlight. I had 12 female cousins and I attribute my awesome dancing skills, what I think is a beautiful singing voice (even though it isn't) and my lack of fear of crowds to them. If you have 12 female cousins, at every event they are putting on shows, playing the piano, they are dressing you up in things I'm not going to mention and they are making you say and do silly stuff. You pretty much lose your fear for stuff like that. You have to have pretty thick skin and not be afraid of too much.

Probably the one thing I'd change in myself… My wife and I talk about this a lot because Sarah says what she thinks right away, which is good, but sometimes it gets you in trouble. I know what I'm going to say every time I open my mouth, but sometimes I don't know when to stop. I think it runs in my family. Sometimes I think I divulge too much. Obviously, writing a book, people are going to know about you anyways, but a lot of people know more about me than maybe they should. This book is just to clarify some of the things they think they know that might not be right.

I've never seen my dad afraid to get up in front of a crowd. The only difference between him and me is that I think he puts general preparation into things if he has to make a speech or something, and we're both good at reading crowds, but I never write notes or speeches or anything. I just kind of wing it, and it seems to work out for me. I'm probably a little more silly and humorous than he is. I think some of the things I've learned from him, and one thing about my dad and me is we're not afraid to make fun of ourselves. If I'm the butt of the joke and people laugh, then that's just as good as someone else being the butt of the joke.

He's funny, but with 12 female cousins, I'm a little more emotional, sensitive and kind of silly funny than he is. I would not call my dad emotional, but when I talk about emotional, I cry at movies. I'm not your stereotypical Midwest guy in that I'm pretty sensitive and not afraid to let it show.

I'm not really afraid of any kind of interaction with any kind of people. When you are a kid traveling in a van with 12 high school players from Harding High School or men or women college players from IPFW on weekends, when you are getting to run around gyms all over the country because your dad lets you go with him, you get a certain level of independence.

Even in college, I was kind of the life of the party. Girls were not attracted to me because I was a handsome guy and God knows we didn't have any money, it was more, ``Who's that guy having the really good time?" I was the guy at every high school dance who had 15 girls dancing with him because the other guys were too cool to dance. I was always the dorky guy dancing. Girls liked to dance, and so did I. I wasn't going to sit there with my hands crossed trying to look cool.

At wedding receptions, I'm always the first one up, and my son is the same way. He loves to dance, and there's nothing wrong with that.

CHAPTER 17

I know a lot of people think I am cocky. I think cocky people are the ones who have no self-esteem and they try to show they do by being cocky. I have a lot of self esteem. I know I am good. I know I am one of the best setters ever to play. That's not being cocky, that's just looking at what I've accomplished over my career.

It wasn't always like that. I'd say early in my career, I was a little cocky, overconfident, because I had not accomplished anything, people were telling me I was good, and maybe I didn't believe it so I was acting that way to maybe show that, yes, maybe they were right.

You can take any great athlete, Jordan, Gretzky, whomever, to be confident all the time is a very difficult thing, especially in sports where the armchair quarterbacks want to talk badly about you, whether you are Peyton Manning or Lloy Ball. You have to have to have kind of an inner peace, an inner confidence so when you reach a certain point in your career you can overcome and block out all those nay-sayers as well as focus on your task at hand to lead your team to a victory. I feel I have that. I don't even look at the game so much as winning and losing any more. I just know that if I play to my capability every point and try to help the players around me do the same thing, the result most of the time will come out the way I want it to be. I think that is confidence.

When I went out to San Diego, I had a lot of animosity built up on the Midwest vs. West thing going on. The West Coast had basically dominated the sport to that point, winning every national championship and then lording it over the rest of the country. I remember USC walking into the Hilliard Gates Center the first time wearing their snazzy Nike outfits. We were lucky to get practice T-shirts at IPFW, and they were dressed in Nike head-to-toe. You could tell they thought their you-

66

know-what didn't stink, and the hard part for a lot of Midwest guys to accept is that they were better. Now, maybe not so much, but then, they were better than us.

Everybody around home talks about us playing UCLA in a great match in 1994 when we lost to them in four games. They were better than us. That automatically causes you to have a chip on your shoulder if you are me or someone else from the Midwest. They have something that you want to have. Once you go out there as an individual, though, things kind of switch. Instead of having to try to prove your team, all you have to do is try to prove yourself. It was not easier, but I found that little motivation of remembering every time they walked into our gym or every time they beat us helped me as an individual strive to beat out all the California setters. I kind of took it personally as this was my chance as a Midwesterner to kind of represent all my former teammates and beat these guys out. It was kind of a moral victory for everybody.

I felt I did have to prove something, and some of those guys out there made you feel that way. Coley Kyman constantly made comments about goats and sheep and farmland and this and that, and wipe your boots off before you come on the court. It was brutal sometimes, but I think in the long run it made me tougher, made me want it even more. Sometimes the harder you get pushed, people either break or they start to push back. I think I pushed back and I think that's why I got to the position I did.

Right away I noticed a difference on the national team. College volleyball players and national team volleyball players are not really the same thing. There are guys who think they are good in college, but really aren't good enough to go to the national team, and they were the guys who really gave me the hardest time. Guys like Bryan Ivie (USC) or Duncan Blackman (Stanford) or Brent Hilliard (Long Beach State) went to the national team, and while they thought California was great, never once threw the Midwest in my face. From Day 1, they knew I must have been good enough to be there. Then you prove it every day that you are and they get even more respect for you.

When I came out West, I was entering a new world, but I never felt intimidated. I think a lot of that has to do with being so comfortable in front of people, and having no fear because of those 12 female cousins. It's kind of the same way on the court playing basketball, playing volleyball. I was never afraid to fail. My job was just to try to do the best I could and have a good time. Even now, I still just try to have a good time. I think coming from a family where you could speak your mind and you could dance if you wanted to, all that helped. My dad was always, ``As long as you play hard, I don't care if you win or lose, I don't care what happens."

I think once you get to the national team level now, a lot of the petty college rivalries, chip on your shoulder, East vs. West stuff is thrown away a little bit. Now I think everyone knows that volleyball is good across the board. I'm sure Marv Dunphy knows.

I don't mean that as a slam on Marv, who is the Pepperdine coach and also coached the 1988 Olympic Gold Medal team, but I think of him as one of those old-school West Coast coaches. Maybe Marv is a little less arrogant than some, but they are confident because they win all the time. When you win all the time, that's just the way you are. People get upset with guys like Al Scates of UCLA, but when you win that many national championships, you are entitled to be confident in your abilities. Now I think maybe they realize they can be a little too overconfident and overlook some teams that are just as good if not better.

For me it was bittersweet when IPFW finally won a match at the final four, beating Pepperdine in the 2007 semifinals because I couldn't be there. I was distraught for about a day and a half when I found out both my sisters were going, and I knew the Fort Wayne contingent would be huge. For about a week I had 60 emails a day from all the alumni who were driving up or flying in for it. I just wanted to be part of that environment. I wanted to be like Loren Gebert was in 1991, jumping off the bench when we won our first MIVA. I wanted to be that guy to jump out of the stands and go run to my dad when they win their first national championship.

The sweet part is I was just so proud of my dad. You know how Arnie is – a month into the season the team is terrible, and then they'll win six in a row and it'll be, ``We're pretty good." Then they'll lose one and it's ``Aw, no, we're no good." He's so up and down, but I could tell when they started going on that streak that he was going to have them up at the right time. It's just a good bunch kids and they played real well together and just represented our school very well. It was just everything a program should be, and for them to have a chance at the final match... there were only two steps left we could take. We just took one, and there's only one left. I really hope that can happen during my dad's tenure at IPFW because he really deserves to win a national championship more than anybody.

I just felt a great sense of pride, even from the other side of the world. The next day I was trying to explain to the guys in my best Russian why I was so happy after the Pepperdine match, and then a few days later why I was so sad. That was interesting as well.

CHAPTER 18

The first time I ever saw Sarah, we were at a bonfire party. A buddy of mine, Jay Miller, heard about it going on outside New Haven on a farm. We were sophomores in college at the time, and Sarah had gone to New Haven High School. Jay Miller, Felipe (Pepa) Ralat and I went out there, and we knew a couple of the guys so we were just having a beer, standing around talking.

This is going to sound very corny and romantic, but I look on the other side of the fire and there are three girls standing there. One of them I knew, which was Jill Eytcheson whose father worked with mine at New Haven. The girl in the middle was tall, skinny with long blonde hair. I was just looking at her, and I asked my buddy Jay if he knew her, and he said he had never seen her before.

We kind of wandered over and introduced ourselves to everybody and I talked to Jill. It turned out they were all freshmen at IPFW that year, and school had just started so I hadn't had a chance to meet everybody yet. We kind of talked, and 10 minutes into the conversation, the police show up in three cars. They are on the megaphone saying, ``Anybody who is under age... if you run you're going to be arrested." We stand there, because I had only had a beer, but Sarah and her friends take off for the cornfields. So that was our first meeting.

The police came up to us and asked us why we didn't run, and we said we had just gotten there. So they said, all right, just go home.

The next Monday at school, we're in Kettler Hall where everyone kind of congregates by the mastodon bones, and sure enough here comes Sarah walking in the front door. Pepa is standing with me and says he's going to go ask her out. I was like, the heck with that, so I kind of step in front of him and ask her out. We're standing on the stairs there, and I say, ``Hey, I met you the other night, do you want to go out and have dinner or something?''

So that's how it started. Our first date was at Cheddars, and I remember she ordered chicken fingers and a salad. We started dating, and we were together until the last three months of my senior year. I knew I was going to join the national team in San Diego, and I didn't know if I loved her enough to take her with me, but I sure as heck knew I wasn't ready to get married, so I decided to break it off and enjoy my last three months of college.

It was a good and bad decision by me. Bad, because I probably did love her, even though I wasn't sure of it. I was 22, but the reasons I broke up with her were not good reasons, certainly not valid ones. They seemed valid at the time. It would have been nice not to have had that little lull in our relationship, but she had never dated anybody before. We were apart eight months before we got back together. Some guys may have a difficult time knowing their wife dated other people or this and that, but it actually gave her the chance to kind of shop around. You hear a lot of bad stories of people married 20 years and all of a sudden the lady is like, ``You're the only man I ever loved, I've ever been with, why didn't I date other people?'' and this and that. This gave her a chance to date other people, and I did, too.

Then after eight months, Ethan Watts figured it out for me. ``Lloy, how come every girl you try to date, all you do is break her down because she's not Sarah? Every time you come home you complain about this girl or that girl because she doesn't measure up to Sarah this way or that way. Why aren't you with Sarah?''

He was right. I remember calling at 3 a.m. trying to find her. I had started at midnight, trying to find her number, and I eventually got a hold of a friend who had her new number. She wasn't in a relationship with anybody, but the first conversation was awkward. I was apologetic about the way things had ended. We had occasionally talked here and there, but that's hard. She was in southern Indiana. She had gone down there to finish school at IU-Southeast. That's where she was when I called her. I had known she dated some other people, some I knew and this and that, but I saw past all that and I just knew. First of all, from the day I ever started liking girls, I knew I wanted tall, blonde – basically Sarah. I called her and I asked if we could try again.

After a break, I came home and she came up here to see her mom and dad. I just said, ``Come with me." She was done with school, and didn't know what she wanted to do but knew she still loved me. So we lived together out there through 1996, and we got engaged right after the Olympics, in September of 1996. Then we went to Japan together, my first year as a professional. I saw her every hour of every day, and I knew after that, ``Good call, this is who I want to get married to."

Sure enough, it's been 15 years now.

When we decided to get married on September 13, 1997, I asked Doug Beal and Jim Coleman a year ahead of time what the schedule was going to be. They said no problem because there were no conflicts. But about two months before the wedding, the NORCECAs got moved and we were going to be in Puerto Rico qualifying for the world championships. They said, ``You gotta be there." I'm like, ``I'm getting married. It's done, it's arranged." It worked out that I would only miss the first two matches against Puerto Rico and Canada, but if I flew the day after my wedding I could get down there in time to play Cuba, which was the match they really wanted me there for.

I agreed to it, but Ethan was in my wedding, Doug says, ``You can't go. You have to come with the team." Ethan says, ``I'm going to the wedding." Doug says, ``Your Olympic future may depend on this decision." Ethan says, ``Now I know I'm going to the wedding."

I'm also going to point out that Ethan was the only guy who did not play in the Olympics, even though he was on the team. Did that have anything to do with it? I hope to goodness no, because Fred Sturm was the coach.

So anyway, the day after my wedding we get up at 5 a.m., Ethan and I and my new bride, and we fly to Puerto Rico and we play that night. We got hammered, of course, 3-0, because Cuba was real good, but that was my honeymoon.

The wedding was right behind the Hilliard Gates Center in the gazebo. We wanted to have an outdoor wedding, and there was a story behind that.

Sarah comes from a stout Catholic family and I grew up Lutheran, Missouri Synod Lutheran, which is pretty hard-line as far as Lutherans go. According to her family, if we're not married in the Catholic church it's not real; my parents wouldn't say that but by the same token I'm sure they'd love for us to be married in a Lutheran church. So we just kind of split the difference and said we're going to get married outside. Then there are no problems. She and I were fine with that.

There was also a cross country meet that day on campus and they had promised it would be done in time for the wedding, but they still had all the markings up. It ended up being beautiful. The gazebo was decorated with flowers, and Sarah was so beautiful. There were about 200 guests, and it was a real nice event. When you have an outdoor wedding, the weather is always in question, but it was a beautiful September day, just the way we wanted it.

I think any athlete's wife has to be pretty special, especially one who has to travel the world, not just like in the NBA going city to city. I'm all over the world, and I know like everybody Sarah had ideas of what she wanted her life to be, but her goal and her dream was to be a great wife to me and a great mother to our children, to support me in every way possible, and that's exactly what she has done. People may not believe it, but Sarah and I have never fought, not one argument. We don't go to bed angry, we discuss everything. At the same time, we have a very good understanding of how our relationship works. Sarah likes me taking care of her. I like her taking care of me and my children. We discuss everything together and try to make the best decision based on what we think is best for our family.

In other words, she lets me feel like I'm in charge.

Dyer was born August 6, 2001, conceived in Italy and born in Fort Wayne and back in Italy when he was 30 days old.

Mya was born July 17, 2006, conceived in Greece and born in Fort Wayne.

A lot of people try to plan this and that, and we were lucky, especially nowadays when people have a difficult time getting pregnant and stuff. We always wanted to make sure we were back home when we had the baby, and God just kind of helped us out with real good timing.

Dyer's name actually came from a movie Sarah and I watched when we were dating, ``Reality Bites.'' Winona Ryder, Ethan Hawke. Ethan Hawke's character was named Troy Dyer, and I remember saying to Sarah over my bowl of popcorn, ``That's an awesome name. We should name a kid Dyer.'' She probably thought I'd forget about it, but I didn't.

With Mya, it was between that or Olivia. It's not really anything significant though we told my sister Amy it was her name jumbled, but it was just a nice name. She knows now.

With all of our names we try to put a ``Y'' in it just because my name has a ``Y'' in it. That's my one egotistical thing, as well as keeping all the middle names James and Jane because of family tradition. Arnie James, Lloy James, Dyer James. We try to keep that in the family a little bit.

Since Dyer was born is when I've had all the success in my career. Being a father I think was one of the turning points in becoming a great setter. It made me realize I shouldn't waste my time frivolously in the gym. I was always in a hurry to get out of there and go back and see my kids so I made time count when I was in there. I also felt like I had something else to play for. It helps you prioritize your life. You can't be selfish like you are as a young athlete when you have kids.

CHAPTER 19

I married a Catholic, and the priest we went to for our pre-wedding counseling basically said she was going to Hell because I was Lutheran. So right there I have my soon-to-be wife crying, she's going to Hell, and I'm just going, ``What is going on?" I got into a little bit of an argument with him. I said, ``I have a really difficult time believing God would look at this woman and who she is and not let her in on a couple technicalities." Catholics and Lutherans – the guy who invented our religion was a Catholic for goodness sakes, Martin Luther. How far off could it be?

Then we went through some more premarital counseling with a pretty hard-line, right-wing Lutheran pastor. In not so many words, he basically told Sarah that unless she changed, she was going to go to Hell.

All those conflicts we went through just made me love her more.

From that point on, I began looking at religion a little differently. I think I have a good faith. It's not like my Mom's faith, for example. I'm not one to preach. I would never condemn or condone someone else's religion. I accept the fact that there are other religions besides mine. My goal in a religion for me and anyone else is to do unto others as you'd like to have done to you, and I believe that there is a God and because of His son I'm going to go to heaven. That's pretty much how I break it down.

A lot of people, and I've listened to my aunts and uncles… there are two different branches of the Lutheran Church – and they argue about this and that, and I look at them going, ``It's the same religion." I mean apples and oranges, wine not wine, body not body… I get frustrated when people lose the point. The only thing my parents and I argue about is religion. I would never try to argue my Mom and Dad's religion even though they are amazed how well versed I am in it, but it's too political sometimes. It's too much red tape. Just go celebrate your faith, and be nice to people. It's a done deal.

That's kind of what Sarah and I believe in. We belonged to a church when we lived in Colorado for a while, but because we've moved so much we've never really tied ourselves to one church. I wouldn't say we attend regularly, but obviously on important occasions on the Christian calendar we attend and whenever it's possible. Our children know about God and know about Jesus. They will. They probably won't go to a parochial elementary school like I did, but we'll make sure they have God in their lives until the point where they choose otherwise.

I think God is the reason why I have the life I have. I also believe it's our hard work together, but that He has guided us in that direction. I'm not a Born-Again. We have Mormons on the national team, we have Born-Agains, we have Catholics, we have Jews, we have everybody, and I'm fine with all of it. I'm fine with Muslims, I'm fine with Hindu. If you look at any religion the principles are the same, and it's the fundamentalists and other people who change that. It's that there is a God, he made the world, he sent a son who died and rose to save us. As long as you believe that, the rest is just something to argue about on Sunday.

The perspective I talk to my Mom and Dad about is that I have seen so much. How can a billion Chinese be condemned to Hell? It's not possible, I don't think. There has to be some kind of connection with all of these religions. I've lived in Italy where it is 99 percent Catholic, I've lived in Greece where it's Greek Orthodox, I've lived in Russia where it's Russian Orthodox. I don't have enough blinders on to condemn all those people. I think God, Muhammad, Allah, whatever you want to call him, is much more compassionate than we are. I think he lets some things slide as long as you're not a nutbag like some of these fundamentalists are nowadays. As long as you follow a couple of principles, I think you are good to go.

That's what my family does.

CHAPTER 20

I always say I'm from Woodburn. I always say I live in Fort Wayne now, but I'm from Woodburn which is about 15 minutes East of Fort Wayne. People have hardly ever heard of Fort Wayne, much less Woodburn, but it's where I grew up. It's where I played Little League baseball, it's where every day after high school I went to Woodburn Park and shot baskets with my buddy Marc Evans. It's where I went to Norm's Supervalu Grocery and everybody knew my name, it's where the Dairy Sweet was after the game to go get ice cream.

We have cornfields on three sides of the school, and it doesn't get much more stereotypical than that. We have FFA Day when kids drive their tractors to school. I don't even know how many high schools offer agricultural classes any more besides us. It's rural, but there's something safe about it. If my kids could grow up and go to school in a safe environment like that, I'll think I've done a good job as a parent.

There was a four-way stop in the middle of town and they have since added a stop light. It's a town of about 2,300 people, a big farm community and a B.F. Goodrich Plant across the road from our old house. My first summer jobs were hoeing beans and de-tasseling corn, and I actually worked at Bob's Restaurant washing dishes in the back. It was my home. I never really thought twice about not saying I was from there. For the most part people treated me well, treated my family well. I felt like part of the community growing up there, much more than I did Fort Wayne.

It's kind of like my Hickory. It's real solid. It's not fake. People were real true, and there's not any kind of political agendas or anything else. It was just a real good place to grow up, and those are getting hard to find.

After the 2004 Olympics I went back and talked to the high school, and that was awesome. They have redone the school and they have a brand new gym, not that crackerbox we used to play in. There's air conditioning on the second level, and we never had that. It seemed so small. Maybe I'm bigger, I don't know.

I talked to the kids, and some of them I probably had their parents in my class. I felt like they were really into it and I was super excited about it. It's one of the most exciting speeches I've gotten to give. Mrs. Etzler, my speech teacher, asked me to come back and do it, and it was awesome. I felt real connected to the kids. I know there's a bunch of generations in between but I felt kind of like a student, like I was back in school again. I felt at home. Even when I go back to Central Lutheran where I went to elementary school, I always feel real close to those kind of places, and Woodlan has a lot of great memories for me. Even though, unfortunately, I wasn't always the most popular person, I enjoyed high school. I really did. It was great to go back and, I think, hopefully shed some light on what the rest of the world is like to those kids.

I run into people all the time I went to school with, more often acquaintances than friends. We started with around 100 kids in my class, but we had a bunch of problems, and I think by the time we graduated we were down to around 87. I think there were only 300 kids in the whole high school.

When I talk in classes, I tell them that I sat there just like them. I went to high school where I had 80 people in my graduating class, and some people never left Woodburn. I did. If you don't want to leave, that's fine, but if you do, it's not a dream, it's a possibility. It's not necessary that your parents have money. My parents sure didn't. My dad was a school teacher, and I wore the same basketball shoes three years in a row even though they didn't fit. You just have to work hard and keep pushing and keep dreaming and make it happen. You see some people's eyes light up, and some don't.

Most of them get it that they live in America. Actually, now most Europeans get it more than Americans do that anything is possible. If you want to work and you are happy at the local fast food, and you love it, that's great. You can do that here. If you want to learn a language, you can do that here. You can do anything here where in Russia you can't do anything. In Greece they don't have money to do that kind of stuff. There may be one university in the whole city. We have how many universities in Fort Wayne alone? Five, six? And the government tries to help financially to make sure that anyone who wants to can go. We take that for granted here, and more than anything that's one reason why Europeans dislike Americans. It's not because we're richer or we're more powerful, but because we take those opportunities for granted and they don't have them. They don't take anything for granted because they don't have them.

Coach Gay Martin was someone who was really close to me during those high school years. Dad was traveling a lot with the team, though he tried to go to every game possible that he could. When I was kind of going through the recruiting process, Coach Martin really helped me. He never tried to push me one way or the other, because it would have been great for him obviously to have a player go to IU, but he always did what was in my best interest. He'd have us over to his house after ACAC championships and stuff, and I spent a lot of time in his office talking about not only basketball, but life and stuff. I think I would have a much harder time socially and academically without some of his guidance.

My family and I go back to Woodburn a lot, and we'll drive around the park and take the kids to play. We'll drive over to Antwerp to the A&W Drive-In and have a chili dog, and then come back to the Dairy Sweet, which football coach Leland Etzler used to own, and hopefully it's lemon day because I love the lemon cone there.

Woodburn doesn't change too much. I don't have my name on a sign there or anything like that, and I wouldn't expect them to. It wouldn't be Woodburn if it was. They would never promote somebody for the wrong reasons. If you ask people, they'll say, ``Lloy is from here. We saw him play basketball at the gym every Friday night, and we've watched him play in the Olympics.'' Hopefully they say he's a nice boy.

I could live anywhere in the world, but I always come back to this area and that's probably the second-most asked question I ever get asked besides, ``Why didn't you go to IU?'' I always say it's because of the people. For the most part, people of the Midwest and Fort Wayne are kind of an extension of Woodburn, just in a bigger city. People are pretty friendly, they are simple folks just trying to have the best life that they can and raise their kids. That's what I want to do.

There are other reasons, too. Some of them are economical. I'm not an NBA guy, and I don't make $10 million a year. I make good money, and it goes a lot further here than it would if I lived in San Diego. If I want to retire in the next few years, if I live in this area, I'd be able to do not much of anything and be OK. If I lived in Los Angeles or Las Vegas or somewhere, I'd have to have a good income still. To be honest, I think about that.

The most important thing of all the reasons is that my Mom and Dad are here and Sarah's Mom and Dad are here. I love my Mom and Dad. I can't put it into words, but I feel differently about each one of them, but the love is exactly the same. I know Sarah is the same way with her parents. To see how they are with our kids, I want my kids to have their grandparents. Her Mom and Dad are great with our kids, so are my Mom and Dad. It's nice to know when I'm here, I can get in my car and in 10 minutes be sitting at my Mom's table, having a coffee with her any time I want. Maybe that's the 12 female cousins again and my sensitivity side coming out, or maybe it's the fact that I love them so much.

Some people have suggested that I come back because I'm still somebody here, and I don't think that's it. People come up and say stuff to me, and I do get uncomfortable with that sometimes, being recognized. It's a little different from being in front of people. I like coming back here because I feel like I fit in. I feel like when I walk into Meijer in my flip flops and T-shirt with my hat on backwards no one looks twice. If I walk into Saks Fifth Avenue like that, they look at me kind of funny. I can't think of anything I own that has a designer label. As far as premium stuff, I like Starbucks I guess, but we've got 10 of those now, too.

Fort Wayne seems like it has always been a good mesh for me. I don't feel like I have to try too hard. I'm a pretty uptight guy sometimes, but when I'm here or up at Angola at the lake, which is basically an extension of Fort Wayne, I don't have too many cares, too many worries. I've always been a Hoosier, I think. Even someday, hopefully long in the future when my Mom and Dad and Sarah's Mom and Dad are gone, I'm not sure we'll move even then. They are a reason why we are here, but the main one is it's who we are.

Ball's exuberance has always made him one of the most popular
players in the world. Courtesy FIVB.

Ball was named the most valuable player at the World League Finals in Brazil three weeks before the Olympics. Courtesy FIVB.

Ball is setting middle hitter Ryan Millar, a three-time Olympian and one of his favorte targets. Courtesy FIVB

From left to right, USA team members Clay Stanley, Reid Priddy, Rich Lambourne, Riley Salmon, Ryan Millar and Lloy Ball.

After being sidelined earlier with a calf injury, Lloy Ball celebrates a key point in the comeback against Venezuela with Ryan Millar, Riley Salmon and Reid Priddy.

Team USA celebrates after winning the gold medal at the Beijing Olympics. Lloy Ball is third from the left in the top row.

After running into the stands following match point in the gold medal match, Lloy Ball hugs his mother Sandy as his son Dyer looks on. Courtesy FIVB

Lloy Ball with his father Arnie after winning the gold medal in Beijing. Courtesy of Lance Adams

Lloy Ball with his wife Sarah and son Dyer and their gold medal. Courtesy Lance Adams.

Lloy Ball, American patriot. Courtesy FIVB

CHAPTER 21

Going to the Olympics is like going to a Club Med for jocks. It's all inclusive, all paid for. There are five McDonald's in the village and you can get whatever you want for free. You can eat any kind of food you want from sushi to steak to pasta, prepared by big-time chefs. You live in glorified student housing, four athletes living in a quad, with kitchenettes. There are a lot of beautiful people who are really in shape from all over the world. Every national team is sponsored by somebody so they are wearing all their free gear, but thank goodness it has their flag on it somewhere so you know where they are from.

It's funny because when you are in the village, it's not a real big deal. There's a lot going on. There's music if you want it or there are training facilities, weight rooms or massage therapists or you can get a hair cut or go to a post office or go to a computer café. It's like its own small little city. To the athletes it's not a big deal because they are all athletes. It's only when you come outside and somebody asks you about it that you realize it is pretty cool.

In Athens during the 2004 games we were sitting there eating and at the table across from us was Allen Iverson eating Big Macs, or in Sydney we were eating and Goran Ivanisevic started talking to us in perfect English. It's not a big deal until all of a sudden you are done with it and you realize these are some pretty big stars.

I met Monica Seles who knew Lindsay Davenport in 1996. Lindsay's father Wink Davenport is one of the best officials in volleyball and I've known Lindsay forever. I've always liked Monica the way she grunts and yells when she hits the ball, so we just sat down at their table and said hi. She's a real nice girl, but obviously very protective, which is understandable.

Unfortunately, the Olympics haven't always been that much fun for me.

The 2000 team was the best Olympic team I played on. We had a 0-5 record, but if anyone in the Olympics had played us three months earlier, we'd have killed them. We were 10-0 in the World League and we were playing awesome, placing fourth in the World Cup six months earlier. And then a month before the games I started having knee problems, and Mike Lambert's shoulder started giving him problems from taking too many swings. I don't blame any of this on Doug Beal, our coach, but we over-trained and played too many matches so we just showed up in bad shape. I got six cortisone shots during that Olympics, and Lambert had a couple. I didn't go to the opening ceremonies because I knew I couldn't walk and then play the next day. I still think if we could have won that first match against Argentina we could have had a chance to get something going, but we had peaked before we got there and we were on the way down by then.

I truly believe it was our best team. We had a big opposite in George Roumain, a big left side in Lambert, a guy on the left side with a fast arm in John Hyden and we had Ryan Millar and Tom Hoff in their prime in the middle with Erik Sullivan at Libero. It was a good team, but going in, instead of going upwards, we all felt that we had already started coming back down, and it was just too hard to stop. In every match we played well one set, and we were never blown out, but they were four sets or five sets that were all real close. We just never had the same energy we had before, and things didn't happen as easily as they happened before.

I was disappointed because I physically couldn't perform the way I wanted to perform. To be honest, I probably shouldn't have played, and we had a good setter backing me up in Chip McCaw. As my knee kept getting worse, I couldn't practice between matches, and he probably should have come in to see what he could do. At least he would have been more mobile than I was.

That was really hard because I was looking forward to it so much after the disappointment in 1996. I'd been on the team for six years, and we'd had a really good quad leading up to it. I was just really frustrated because I felt like this was going to be a big coming out party for USA volleyball, and it just didn't happen. I couldn't do anything to help, and I just felt real helpless.

CHAPTER 22

I needed surgery on my knee after the 2000 Olympics, but I ended up waiting because I had a big contract waiting in Italy. I had to be there a month after the Olympics, and if I'd have had the surgery, they would have cancelled the contract. So I just went over and gutted through it. I'm glad I had great players around me and somehow we got to the semifinals. We lost, but I played good enough to get asked to stay, and that summer I came back home and had the knee surgery.

That first year was hard because I was with a bunch of older Italian guys who couldn't or didn't want to speak English, but I had a coach who did so he was basically telling me everything in English which kind of upset those old guys. The one thing about Italy is that they don't supply translators so you have to learn Italian, but I didn't learn any that first year because of the security situation.

Up to that point, I had not really proven myself too much other than in 1994 at the World Championships, so I had to really bust my hump and show what I was made of, and I finally earned the approval of the Italian players. Some of the guys knew something wasn't quite right with me, but some days it wasn't too bad, and some days walking was difficult. If it wasn't too bad, sometimes it felt normal. The meniscus was slowly deteriorating, and sometimes if the tracking was off, you'd just bite your tongue and get through it. I had a dime-sized hole in my meniscus and every time you'd bend your knee sometimes it would catch and just give out. I'd go to jump and a lot of times I was just jumping off one leg. Sometimes I could jump off two feet, but sometimes it looked like I was jumping sideways and of course it was a lot lower. I never knew until I bent the knee, and I kept jump serving.

It worked out where the coach got into some trouble and they ended up firing him so it took all the attention off my physical problems. I never told anybody what was going on. When I came back the next year, everybody was like, ``What in the world happened to you? This is what we thought we were getting." I told them I had a little bit of a knee problem, but I lied a bit and told them it ended up being a little bit more than I thought it was. So we had a new coach and a new setter basically, and we won so I got another two-year contract after that.

Up until recently, I would have said the Italian League was the best in the world. It's basically 12 all-star teams, and I try to tell people that the last-place team has an Olympic gold medalist on it so every Sunday is a dogfight. All the best Brazilian players play in Italy. All the best players from the Yugoslavian team that won the 2000 gold medal played in Italy. All the best Russians up until a few years ago played in Italy. The volleyball is the best technically, the coaches are the best and are much more tactically sound. They put a lot of time and energy into it so the players respond. They tell the players to do something and they have a technical reason why you should do it.

This is basically like the NBA in Europe. Every match is televised, we play in 7,000-seat stadiums and we use big busses, big planes and we get big contracts. There's a whole newspaper dedicated just to volleyball. There's men's or women's volleyball on television every night, and where else does that happen?

You only play on Sundays, and the rest of the week you train unless you play in the Champions League and then you play on Wednesdays, too. It's nice as you get older because Monday you have off, Tuesday you lift weights, Wednesday you finally touch a ball, Thursday you do both, Friday you have one big practice, Saturday you goof around and Sunday you play the match.

The Italian season lasts eight months, and there are 12 teams so you play each of them home and away. Then you have quarterfinals that are two out of three matches and then the semis and finals are three out of five. My team always went at least as far as the semis all four years.

My second year we had a year under our belts and we knew each other. It's real hard to put together a team and then win in that same year. The second year my Italian got a little bit better and guys felt more comfortable with me on and off the court so we were a tighter unit. I knew who could kill the ball at key points and who couldn't. I truly believe it takes two years to win and you can't be together after three.

So the next year we play in the Champions League, too and we went to the finals and lost to Belgorod, a Russian team, in Milan. Then we went to the finals again in the Italian League and lost so we had two second places. In Modena, winning is all-important, but that was still a pretty good year.

My fourth year is why I go by the philosophy that it takes two years to win and you can't be together more than three. We were together for too long. All of a sudden stuff you've let slide for a few years, in your fourth year you aren't going to let it slide any more. It just went downhill in a hurry. We actually had a winning year and won the second division European title to salvage a little bit of the season, but we didn't even make the playoffs in the Italian League. I was home by April 15 that year.

I played in Italy up until 2004, and then I thought I was going to retire after the Olympics so I didn't sign a contract again. Then a Greek team talked to me after the Olympics and it was more money than I had made in Italy and I got to play with two Americans in a place where it was warm all the time. My wife was like, ``Sign it!''

CHAPTER 23

I don't have any choice but to go to Europe if I want to play professionally and make my living at what I love to do. I could go to South America, but I'm not sure they like us any better down there, so if I want to make the most money I possibly can, that's where I have to be.

As an American who plays and works overseas, my philosophy is ``Defend your president and country at all times." That's what it feels like sometimes, too. Every day the polls show people like us less and less, and whether you are a Democrat or Republican, like Bush, don't like Bush, like Clinton, don't like Clinton, I feel you are an extension of your president. Even though I know he doesn't talk to me when he makes his choices, the Europeans blame me for it.

It's just part of being an American when you live and work overseas. We're under the microscope. America is the Michael Jordan of the world in economics, politics and everything, and everyone judges themselves by us. They like to poke fun and ridicule us when we do something, especially when it doesn't work out, that they don't like.

I'm a Republican. I vote Republican, but I have no problem if our president might be a Democrat as long as they do a good job. I thought Clinton was a fine president. I found it comical when he had Lewinskygate that Europeans loved that. They could care less about scandals and things like that because he was awesome for foreign policy and the environment, and that's what they care about. I kind of lean that way, too.

I'm not such a staunch or right-side Republican. I don't agree with what Clinton did, but I think he was a good president, just like I don't care what George Bush does in his private life as long as he leads the country. That's his job. That's what we pay him for. If he does this on the side, does that on the side, that's between him and his wife and his family. That's their problem. Our job should only be to make sure he's doing the best for our country when he's in the seat.

Whether the president is a Democrat or Republican, right or wrong, I defend him. I didn't vote for Clinton, but I didn't have a problem with him. Once he's in, he's in. That's what upsets me with what's going on now, whether you like him or not, people are leaving our guy out to hang. Now is the time when he needs support the most.

When you are in Europe, you find yourself trying to answer questions, like, ``Why isn't Al Gore president?" ``Is Jeb Bush helping his brother become president in Florida?" and this and that. No matter what they say, it's basically always negative against America, whether it be foreign policy, or if this is a war about oil or whatever.

I found myself kind of under the gun and getting asked a lot of questions that most of the time I didn't know the answers to. I say, ``Look, this is my president," because they don't do that a lot any more. They just don't support Italian Prime Minister Silvio Berlusconi. They could care less about him. And Russians, if President Vladimir Putin does something right or wrong, they don't care. They'd much rather make fun of what Bush is doing or what Clinton did and poke fun at us from across the pond.

I never bring up politics overseas, and I actually don't return fire too much until it hits a nerve, especially with Jamie being in Iraq. Once they start talking bad about the soldiers… I even let them talk badly right now about the war, because I don't agree with every reason why we are there. I let them give their opinion, but once they start condemning the soldiers, I put a stop to that. The same thing with Clinton, when some of the guys were making fun of this or that with Lewinsky, calling him names and such… if you assault my president, whether I voted for him or not, that's personal.

I think as this book will show, I'm a patriot, and when you are on foreign soil, you have to stick up for what is yours, and it's not always easy sometimes when they are booing you, throwing pennies at you, throwing batteries at you and everything else. They had to stop announcing I was from America one time in Greece. Off the court friends are OK, and we get into arguments sometimes, but when it's all said and done we pay the bill and go home. But when they have to wheel in plastic covers for your bench because people are throwing things at you like lighters and coins, when they are burning the American flag or hanging Bush in effigy outside, you have to be pretty thick-skinned.

Luckily, it's never been too bad when I've been on the USA team. It's more of a problem on a club team where they feel like there are only one or two Americans so they know there's not going to be too much of a reaction or upheaval about it. It gets a little scary sometimes.

You just have to be careful. I don't wear the USA garb when I'm out and around in Europe. It's one thing when you are with the USA team and you have 15 guys who are all 6-8, and people don't do too much. But if you are one guy with a wife and kids and you have the big USA jacket on, then you are drawing attention to yourself.

European fans are so different from ours. Here in the states we tend to sit on our hands, but overseas the fans like to be hands on, really hands on. They like to throw things, spit, yell stuff, and fight. Greek fans are the worst. They would stop matches because of violence. Fans would tip over buses, throw flares, batteries, lighters and coins.

There was an incident in Athens once where someone approached my wife who was at the game with Dyer when he was real young. He started yelling. It wasn't political, just him hating our team, but he kind of gave her a shove and said, American this and that. I was off the court and into the stands faster than I've ever moved. I ran up there and threw him down because Sarah was so afraid she was crying and screaming. The police came right away and got the guy out of there.

This was a common thing over there. Volleyball is just more popular there, and I was most recognized in Greece and Italy. Whenever my family and I were out on walks, people would want to talk about the last game or other sporting events or ask for pictures and autographs. It's not at all like here except maybe in Fort Wayne where people know me, but otherwise I am just a real tall guy that people think plays basketball.

We're not well-liked overseas. International volleyball does not have the security like the NBA or NHL has. Sometimes we're on our own, and it gets nerve-racking. After September 11 happened, we were in Modena, Italy, and the team wouldn't let me do any more interviews for a couple of months. They took off their website that I was from the USA. It was a fear of something happening to an American who is now well-known there. They didn't want people to know that there was a ``big-time'' American living in the city. That was an eye-opening experience, too. I got a letter saying I had to register in Rome and let the embassy know I was there so they could send me updates. Going from Woodburn to this is not exactly the same thing.

I was scared about going to Athens for the 2004 Olympics, and I didn't take my family because of that fear. I truly believed that something was going to happen there, but I went anyway. I just prayed and hoped. I really thought something was going to happen, and that's why I didn't let Sarah and Dyer come. Sarah and I talked about it a lot, and you can't live your life in fear for yourself, but I was not going to put my child in danger. Also, it's my country and if I don't go, what would happen if Jamie said he didn't want to go? That's not quite the same thing because I'm on a much lower level, but it's kind of similar.

I was one of the few athletes who would talk publicly of their concerns about the 2004 Olympics and security at that time, and it made a lot of people uncomfortable. Before every Olympics, they have a big media forum somewhere, and before Athens it was in New York City a month before the games. I went as a representative of men's volleyball, and at that time the whole conversation was about 9/11 and the threat of terrorism at the games. People probably don't realize this, but we are media trained, especially when they know someone is not real comfortable or not really in tune to what is happening around the world. Luckily, I'm blessed with my father's genetics when it comes to public speaking, and I know how to use a little B.S. here and there.

You could see the other athletes were uncomfortable talking about this. They were coached into saying, ``We're not concerned because we know what a great job the USOC is doing, and how Greece is really prepared." The whole time I'm thinking, ``That is the exact right thing to say," but anybody who knows me knows I normally don't say the exact right thing. So then they asked me, and I said, ``Yes, I am concerned, not because I think the Greeks are incapable of securing it, not because I don't think the USOC did a poor job of organizing everything, it's just that if crazy people want to do crazy things, there's always that chance, and I'm not willing to take that chance with my wife and son. This is something personal that I am trying to accomplish. If I want to put myself at risk, I feel the rewards out-weigh the risks, but not for my four-year-old son or my wife. My decision to do this shouldn't impact their lives if, God forbid, something happens."

They had all the volleyball people up on stage together, me, Erik Sullivan, Tara Cross-Battle, Stein Metzger, Mysti May, and when I'm talking there are about 200 journalists and it's just dead silent. You could see the other people on the panel looking at me thinking, ``I hope to gosh I don't have to answer a question like this." You could even see the ones who said they weren't concerned bobbing their heads like, ``Yeah, we probably could have said that, too, but we took the safe road."

People were taken aback. There was a big Associated Press story on it and it went through all the papers across the nation. It wasn't like, ``Lloy is throwing up his hands yelling he's nervous," but there are concerns. Usually they want us to be the cucumber cool athletes with all the right answers, but we're still kids and we get scared and we have responsibilities to other people, too. I felt like that was a safe forum to express my concerns.

As for the official reaction, I think the USOC has learned you can only get the athletes to do and say so much, and then they're going to be themselves. It was just before my third Olympics, so I think they were going to cut me a little slack.

The overall reaction was positive. All the papers carried both sides, saying some athletes aren't concerned whatsoever. There are one or two athletes like Lloy Ball who are concerned, and that's why he's not taking his son and his wife over there. It wasn't blown out of proportion. I just think it was a good idea for people to know that not everybody was real comfortable with the situation.

I'm kind of used to dealing with similar situations because our unpopularity is pretty universal in Europe. In France we are super-not popular obviously. This basically happens in places that are not real politically stable themselves. Italy goes through presidents so much they don't even serve through a full term most of the time. Greece is in a coup all the time. In Russia it was OK, believe it or not, because Putin is pretty stable. He isn't going anywhere.

Talking about politics is more commonplace over there. It's like our gossip. In Europe, politics is their Hollywood gossip. What Rumsfeld is doing, what Bush is doing, what Colin Powell's chances are to be president, what Hillary is doing and will Bill be pulling her strings… all that stuff that I think a small percentage of people in America really talk about. There, that's kind of their dinner fodder.

I'll be the first to admit I was politically ignorant up until maybe the age of 28. I voted Republican to that point because my parents voted Republican, and that's a terrible reason to vote that way. About the last seven years I started forming my own opinions, my own ideas. I followed CNN, I followed Fox News because they are different spectrums, reading the paper, reading on the internet, watching debates… I'm not a guru or in love with it, but I feel it's my obligation to be informed. If I go over there and I'm uninformed about the topics, that just feeds their fire. So I try to be as politically intelligent and as informed as I possibly can so when the occasion arrives I can defend it properly.

The hardest thing is when it goes from politics to love to all these cultures, they are much more animated than we are. If you had ever watched me when I speak Italian, my hands are going a mile a minute, but not as much when I'm speaking English. It's just part of the cultural differences. I remember an argument, I'll say a discussion, with some of my teammates, where one of them is standing up pointing his finger at me and shaking it in my face, and I'm up giving him the off the chin and we all sat down and had a different conversation. It's just their passion for life, for love, for food, for politics. If you came to a dinner for our team, and there are 12 of us talking, you'd think we were fighting or that I maybe called someone's mother a bad name, but we could simply be talking about clothes or how bad the pizza is. It's just so passionate with so many hand gestures and the inflection in the voices, that's how it is, and politics is just a favorite topic of theirs.

Luckily, now in my career, people know my stance, and that I'm not a radical. If I was some young Democratic or Republican radical who was doing nothing but causing political trouble, teams wouldn't take me. I'm not that guy. I don't talk too much about it unless someone throws it in my face, but then I'll be quick to defend country and president.

CHAPTER 24

We were living in Modena when 9/11 happened. It was late afternoon and I remember I was in the car with some teammates because we were going to a preseason game in Parma which is about 45 minutes away. I got a call from my agent, and this was during my second year in Italy so my Italian wasn't great yet, but he was talking to me like, ``Did you see, did you hear?" and I was like what? ``The Twin Towers," and I swear to God I thought he was talking about the Houston basketball team with Hakeem Olajuwon and Ralph Sampson. I didn't understand at all what he was saying. Finally, he was like, ``Call Sarah."

We had CNN at the house, so I call Sarah and ask her to turn on the TV. Sure enough, she says, ``Oh, my God, Lloy." I'm on the phone for about 30 minutes, and she basically just has the phone up to the TV. We've got the radio on in the car to the information stations and my Italian teammates are trying to translate for me.

We get to the game and I'm shocked. I haven't seen any visuals yet so this is all just from my wife telling me what has happened. I'm the only American on the team, and the coach says, ``You don't have to play if you don't want." Before the game they took a moment of silence already, and I just sat stunned on the bench for an hour. Finally, we get out and I rush home and just watch TV for probably 12 hours straight. I'm just wondering if we knew anybody. It was so surreal the first time seeing the plane flying into the building. I almost didn't want to think it was true because I didn't want to believe it.

We tried calling back home and all the lines were tied up already. Half the team came to our house to see if we were OK, and the support we got from the people there was amazing. I finally got through to my folks the next morning. I didn't sleep, but the next morning, American time, the lines to the States were back open. My dad was just telling me what was going on and I talked to my sister Amy. I just basically kept watching it on television.

It was even scarier because I had been in Italy for two weeks now, training with the team, but some American players were coming later like Mike Lambert, my teammate from the national team. He had left the day before and flew through New York. A couple of guys were supposed to leave a couple days after, and of course that got postponed. That's when the reality of it sets in, to know that 24 hours difference and your best buddies might not be around any more.

It was strange because everybody took it inward a little bit. It was almost like you didn't want to talk about it. It wasn't a fear, but I didn't want to talk about it because then it might happen again. You know how you talk about something so much that it ends up happening? I didn't want that to happen again. When was the last time we had an attack on our own soil? Pearl Harbor?

I felt a lot of hatred. I like to think I'm a person who sees past ethnicity, race and religion but there was good time when, if I saw someone who might be of Middle East descent, I had some thoughts go through my head that normally don't go through. As wrong as that is, I know… For someone to have so much hate to do that to people who are innocent… you know, it's not a plane of soldiers.

That was the one year where we had a lot of people come over to visit us and we just kind of stayed in all the time. We didn't go out or travel much. The team was very close to me during that year. I had constant calls from team officials, coaches and teammates. When we went to airports, I didn't have to take out my American passport because they kind of checked things through beforehand.

There was just a feeling of helplessness to all of it even though I had no relatives who lived in New York, and I didn't have anybody on the flights. Anytime something of this extreme happens, even though there's nothing I could have done about it… I had a similar feeling with Katrina or the shooting at Virginia Tech. When stuff happens in ``your backyard," meaning America, and you are so out of touch with it because of a lack of information, or language, it's really difficult.

I never heard about the Virginia Tech thing until one of my teammates told me about it. That's when things like that and September 11 are even more shocking than if I had been in America. I'd have been watching it on ABC or CNN or whatever, or I could go on a drive or I could have Mom and Dad come over to talk about it and get together to work out your emotions. When it's just you, your wife and an infant, the two of you are just basically staring at each other like there's no outlet, there's no way to reach out. Then try to converse about it or explain it to people who are not even of your own culture, it's such a helpless feeling. That's how Sarah and I felt. You're just watching it over and over and over again knowing you don't have anyone to reflect on it with or to bounce things off of.

It was just a very guarded year, a year I really didn't enjoy very much. I thought about not going back, but I felt like Sarah said, that we didn't really give it a fair shake because we had a new baby and we had 9/11 so we weren't ourselves the whole year and didn't leave the house much. Luckily, we won the championship in that second season, and it was at the end of the second year and the third when I really started learning Italian because the first two years I really didn't put myself in social situations to learn it.

That second year made Sarah and I closer. Fortunately, terrible things that happen always have a positive effect. It made our country closer, and it made me and my wife closer, just realizing how fortunate and lucky we are. Unfortunately, those things slowly dissipate like it has with our country. Luckily, our feelings have not dissipated.

When we got back for the third year, it was almost like it never happened. They were back to announcing I was from America and it was listed in the program. There were a lot more peace flags up on people's houses and things like that, but there was no more increased security. The consulate quit sending us updates when there might be a protest. It felt like it didn't even occur.

One nice thing about it, and I think this relays what kind of great relationship Italy has with Americans for the most part, in Rome in Vatican City there were many times where there were vigils at night. Seeing that on TV, seeing thousands and thousands of Italians show respect for a different people and the wrong that had been done them made you feel good.

For a short period of time until this last war, I think Europeans treated Americans better than they had in the past. There was some empathy and sympathy for Americans because we were being unfairly targeted. Unfortunately, I think that has changed and gone back in the other direction. I think September 11, for a horrific act, brought the world closer together. It brought our country closer together, and I think it shed a light on how cruel, even though we're the super power, people can be to others who really didn't deserve it just to make a political point. I think people in Europe saw the silliness, the stupidity in it and it brought all those people, not to our side, but to feel for us. They had some emotion for us, and Sarah and I felt that from them for sure.

Now it's back the other way because of the war in Iraq.

CHAPTER 25

Going to Athens for the Olympics was special because there's where I started in 1994 at the World Championships with the bronze medal. When I was thinking about retirement, I thought that would be the perfect place to end, coming full circle, hopefully with a medal. That would make 10 years as the starting setter with the U.S. team.

I felt real good about the team. I knew it would be tough to win the gold medal because the Brazilians had just been so dominant, but we had just come from a match in Texas where we had beaten Russia and we'd had some success against Italy throughout the quad. We were in a nice pool where, if we played some nice volleyball, we knew we could be in good shape. There was Austria, who we had beaten a lot, Holland who we played well against and enough teams that we knew we could win against so that if we could get one other one, we knew we could advance. After we lost the first match to Italy, we got a huge monkey off our backs after going 0-5 in Sydney by beating the Netherlands. After we lost to Russia, we beat Australia to earn a spot in the medal round and then had to face Brazil to finish off pool play.

The only bad thing about our next match was that Brazil threw the game to us. They played most of their guys but they threw the game because if they had won, they would have played the winner of Russia-Italy for the semifinals. If they lost, then they'd have to play the winner of Greece-USA. They were purposely serving out of bounds and hitting balls into the stands. Unfortunately, it worked out for them, but it was just bush league and I said it in a couple of interviews after the match and got a lot of heat for it, but it was bush league and I lost a lot of respect for some of their guys. A couple of their big guys didn't play in that match because they wouldn't be part of it, but it was obvious to everybody what was going on.

So we get to the quarterfinals, and it works out well for us, too, because we probably would not have gotten to the final four if we had to play Russia or Italy in the quarterfinals. We played Greece who we matched up pretty well with. We were in Greece, but sometimes that's not a bad thing, especially when some of the Greek players are not known for having such tough skins. But they have always played well against me, and sure enough, I can't side out. I'm not sure it was anything I was doing, but we weren't serving real well and they were playing real well.

When I got pulled, I think it showed the difference in me playing in my third Olympics. It was the right thing to do. It was the thing we didn't do a couple of other times in other Olympics where I probably should have got taken out. Other players get taken out, too. I'm not going to play great all the time, and Doug made the right call.

When I came out in the fourth game, I was real concerned. It was 12-20, and I'm not going to lie, I thought we were done. When it got to be about 16-21, I was sitting next to Ryan Millar on the bench, and I said, ``We're going to win this set."

Donnie Suxho played great. Competing against Donnie and with Donnie, we were rivals and this and that, but when we're playing a game, we're a team. He played great, and gave us the spark we needed to come back and win 25-23.

Knowing this was my last Olympics, I just decided I wasn't going to be a jerk. I wanted to play, but I was going to support Donnie and jump around, and as the score got closer I jumped even more. I got the rally towels going. I stayed warm in case they needed me to come in and do something. At the beginning of the fifth set, I go over to Doug and say, ``Donnie's going to keep setting, isn't he?" and he said, ``Yes." I just said, ``If you want me to serve or something I'm ready."

I tell people coming in during that fifth set and serving those two points is one of the proudest moments of my career because it's not Lloy Ball-like, to be honest. I always think of myself as a front-runner or as a starter, as a team player not as a leader team player. That role I filled there was as a bench player team guy. I came in to serve when we were down 12-10 and I came up with a dig and we get a good set on the left side for a kill. After a time out, I come back and serve an ace, and the third serve I get in, too, and we take the lead 13-12. It helped give us the momentum and we won the set 17-15 to take the match and advance to the semifinals.

Then we played Brazil in the semifinals and got waxed. They were just a lot better than us, to be honest.

So we were getting ready to play Russia for the bronze medal, and Erik Sullivan and I were up almost all night talking about how we had just played these guys a month ago, and we knew we could play with them. He said, ``Lloy, if they don't serve well, we will win."

Then they hit like 19 aces, and we lost.

There were a couple of questionable calls late in the final game. They called me for being over the net on a set at game point of the second game where I had two hands on the ball. I've still never seen that call happen again. They got a couple calls on aces down the line in the third game. I've never had much success with that Korean ref.

I wasn't disappointed in the match because we had played so hard, and we played so hard in the entire tournament, but I knew I was done. I went into the locker room, and, of course someone had already gone in and set out some beers for everybody, and I just walked in, picked mine up and went into the shower. They had those little seats you can fold down, and I just sat there. I didn't even take a sip of the beer, I just sat it down on the floor and kept saying out loud to myself, ``That was it, that was it." I started to cry a little bit, and then I got done with that and I walked back out and everyone kind of knew and I got some handshakes and hugs and we tried to be as manly about it as we could.

When we came in fourth, you are going home with the exact same thing as if you finished eighth, but it was nice after two disappointing Olympics to have one where at least we were competing for a medal. In hindsight, it probably won't mean a whole lot to me later on because it wasn't a medal. Especially these last five or six years, winning so much in club play, it would just be an awesome thing to finish my career on a good note with a medal so I could give it to my Dad. Not that I want to validate myself or my career, but I've put in so many hours and so much hard work with USA on my back, that I almost think I deserve it. Maybe that's the wrong way to look at it. People can knock me for maybe not playing well or for this or for that, but I don't think that anyone has put more time and energy into it than I have. They sure haven't wanted it as badly as I have. We don't always get what we want, but it sure would be a heck of a nice way to finish up.

CHAPTER 26

After the 2004 Olympics, I thought I was retiring to come back to be an assistant coach at IPFW. I had already talked with my Dad and gotten things worked out where I was going to be the assistant until Dad didn't want it any more and then I would become the head coach.

For some reason I didn't feel as tired as I thought I would after all those years. I just felt good, and the club Iraklis in Greece came up with more money than I had seen, plus I got the opportunity to play with Clay Stanley and Tom Hoff. At this point, I had never played with another American player in seven years of club volleyball overseas, so that was exciting. Tom's wife and my wife are friends, we'd get to play in a beautiful place, Greece, where a lot of people speak English. Sarah and I talked about it, and Dyer was still young enough not to be in school, so I said, ``All right, let's play a year and see what happens."

Sure enough we win the championship and we finish second in the champions league, so they say I have to come back and they give me more money. We liked it, so I did. I ended up playing two years there.

As a team sport, most people only know if you win the gold medal in Olympics, but I've been lucky enough to win a lot of personal awards. And to be honest, I don't care. My dad gives me a hard time because I don't keep many awards, but the feeling of winning is the only trophy I want. Getting paid to win is a good award, too.

For some reason in my mid-30s, I'm playing the best I've ever played We won five cups in two years in Greece, we finished second twice in the champions league, I was the MVP of the champions league, MVP of the Greek league, so I'm like, let's just keep cashing in, I guess.

I was still going to retire, but my agent was just going nuts. ``Lloy, they must hear you say retire because every time the money just keeps going up.'' This is when the Russian league started to get big. Luckily for me, in both the champions league final fours in 2004-05 and 2005-06, we play Belgorod, which was the reigning Russian champion who we had lost to previously on my Italian team. We drew them both times in the semis and we beat them both times, and this was televised all over Russia. Even though people knew me from the U.S. national team, a lot of them were now seeing me first-hand and the calls started coming. I mean offers came from Moscow, from St. Petersburg, from Kazan. ``How much do you want?''

Russia has always been big in volleyball, but now with all this money they have from natural gas, coal and oil, all these Russian billionaires need somewhere to get their money going, so basketball and volleyball teams get it. We have one sponsor for a team with a $4 million payroll.

The money was just too good to turn down. It's as close to $1 million as a volleyball player ever gets. I only signed for one year because it was Russia and second because there was so much money I figured there was no way I would get it all. So even then I told my agent, ``I want a third of it before we even get on the plane.'' The next day it's in my account. I'm like, these guys are serious, I better play well.

We get over there and Russia is everything people say it is. It's cold and there's a lot of snow. The people are not overly friendly, but nice enough. They are just hard-working folks trying to make a buck in a place where making a buck is hard unless you've got a big hole somewhere out there where there's oil in it. The food is real bland, and the seafood is real bad. There's a lot of lawlessness. Police will pull you over and stop every third car to see if they can get a handout. ``We won't give you a ticket if you give us $20'' type of thing. The team gives us a card that gets us through all of that.

But the volleyball is awesome. There are about 300 huge Russian guys who know how to play, and then you throw two foreigners on each team and the league is real good. If you want to see some jump serving and spiking, come up to Siberia in the Russian league and you'll see it.

There are 12 teams in the league. Most of them are around Moscow. For a couple of the teams in Siberia, the players live and train in Moscow and fly to Siberia for their home matches.

I play for Dynamo Kazan which is owned by one of the top five natural gas companies in Russia. Kazan is about 1,600 kilometers east of Moscow, a big city of 1.5 million people, 90 percent of whom are Muslim. It's known for having just a lot of money. Travis Best played on the basketball team there two years ago that won. The ice hockey team two years ago was the Russian champions. Now they have their first Russian champion volleyball team.

We kind of worked it out where they called me and told me they needed an opposite, too, so I could bring whomever I wanted. I said, ``I have this guy who is pretty good. I've played with him for two years now." So Clay Stanley came with me.

The season started in October, 2006, and we played 11 matches in the regular season, but you end up playing more matches during the playoffs than you do in the season. We finished third and had to play the defending champions in the first round of the playoffs, and we beat them three straight. Then we won our semifinal series in five matches. We were cruising in the finals against Dynamo Moscow, leading 2-0 when I threw my back out with a pinched nerve and had to miss two matches. Each match in the finals is best-of-five, and they had a chance to win it at our place in the fourth match. They were up 2-0, but our guys rallied to win the match in five games and force a fifth match in Moscow. It was just a pinched nerve, but I sucked it up and put the belt on to play in the fifth match. There were 7,000 fans at the match, including about 1,000 from Kazan, and we won 3-0.

It's the first volleyball title Kazan has won and they went nuts. When we arrived back at about 1 a.m., the prime minister had tanks sitting at the airport for us to ride on, and there were about 500 people waiting for us with champagne and flowers. There was nowhere to put the glasses, so they just told us to throw them on the runway. Heaven forbid if our flight the next morning had run over them.

After the little party, four hours later I got on the plane to come home. The flights to Fort Wayne ended up taking 20 hours. Luckily, one nice thing about getting better contracts over the last 12 years is that I always get business or first class. It's tough for a 6-8 guy to sit in coach. My kids are spoiled because they have never ridden in coach.

I signed another one-year contract to go back. Sarah and I keep saying, ``This is the last year," but the money is always bigger and the teams are always good.

Now we're the reigning champions, and we'll be in the Champions League again. It's the biggest tournament in Europe for men's and women's volleyball. Depending on how good your league is, one or two teams from every country that has a championship is in this big-money tournament. There are usually 24 teams, six pools of four and you play home and away. Then the best eight teams have the playoffs.

It's good and bad. Last year was good because I only had to play every Sunday except for the playoffs. But this year because I'm going by myself, it will be nice to have the extra game because it will make it go faster. And, I have three second places in the Champions League. I have to win the darn thing. If I win that, there will be no one who will have done what I have done as far as club play. Nobody has won three different titles like I have in Russia, Greece and Italy.

CHAPTER 27

I've visited 42 countries and filled four passports, and in all of those pages had to be added so it's probably more like six to eight normal passports. I've basically been everywhere in the world except Africa, and flying sucks, and you can quote me on that! I have a gold card with United, American, Delta, Lufthansa and some airlines you have never heard of, but even with the benefit of now flying first class, it is still the most physically demanding part of my job. Flying 20-plus hours on a plane and then having to play the next day at a high level is the toughest part of my life.

Here are some tips I've learned to use the hard way.

* Many people think staying up the night before and then sleeping on the flight is a good thing, Wrong! It doubles the effect of jet lag. Get a good night's sleep before traveling, otherwise your future is very groggy.

* Drink water! I drink anywhere from a liter to a gallon of water on trips. Jet lag is more dehydration than sleep deprivation so stay away from the alcohol and pound the water. Yes, you will make 10 trips to the bathroom, but it will pay off when you land.

* Know your time zone. If you need to be alert when you get in, such as for a practice or a meeting, don't go heavy on the airplane food. Now, most flights recommend such things, but eat the salads, chicken and no sweets. If you can sleep when you get in, then you can eat the pasta dishes.

* Sleep. If I am going to arrive early morning and don't want to conk out when I get there I will sleep on the plane. I'll use a sleep aid like Zanex, Ambien or Tylenol PM. Sleeping on a flight is difficult for me because I am usually uncomfortable most of the time, especially when I am playing with the USA team because they are cheep and we fly economy. I'm 6-8, trying to sit in economy – you do the math.

* To help with muscle fatigue, I get up and walk around the plane every two or three hours. I usually go to the back and bother the stewardess, and then I'll find a little spot to stretch and do little movements to get my blood flowing. Plus, I'll get more water from the flight attendants.

* Socks. Now this may seem a little gross to some, but let me say first that my feet do not smell.

I take my socks and shoes off when the flight is long. Feet and knees are the areas most affected during a long flight because all the blood rushes to these spots and stays. That is why it is so difficult to move after flying, and tight shoes and the bands of your socks are the prime suspects so I remove them. Only rarely will someone complain about it, and after I explain the reasons, most join me. Some don't.

* As for the time in between flights, most of the long part in my travel in the airports. Layovers in Istanbul, Milan, Dallas… wherever. I never sit down during layovers unless it is at a time when I need to sleep. I keep moving and keep stretching because blood flow is key.

Sometimes you just have to get off the plane and play, and there's nothing that can be done about it. That's a perfect example of it's more mind over matter. Now matter how much you do on the plane, your body is going to be brutalized. My knees are going to be swollen from flying. My ankles are going to be twice their normal size, and I'm going to be sleep-deprived even if I did sleep because the time zone change and the lighting change. It basically comes down to for that one game you have to suck it up and just accept the fact that you are not 100 percent. That happens, not just with jet lag, but with a lot of things. You walk off the plane and the coach wants you to practice or stretch or get a little sweat going, and all you want to do is find the nearest bed and lay down. You've had terrible airplane food so you've probably got digestion problems, and you're urinating all the time from all the water you drank on the plane. There's nothing comfortable about it, and then having to go and play, it's just one of those times where you just have to buckle down and just do it anyway.

Usually we've got at least three or four days after traveling before a competition. With the USA team, we often get there a week or two ahead of time, and with the club teams, they try to get you there at least 48 hours ahead of time. Traveling in Europe, it's usually just a three or a four-hour flight, which isn't bad. It's when you get into 20-plus hours of travel, then it's too tough. Every time I go to Europe it's more than 20 of travel. On my last trip to Russia, there was a 12-hour layover so the whole trip took about 40 hours. Going to China will be 36 hours, Japan is about 24 hours or more. Flying time that's 12 to 14 hours, but then you have airports and layovers and bus travel, and that's what kills you.

For the Olympics, the opening ceremonies will start August 8 in Beijing, and unfortunately the World League doesn't end this year until the last week of July so I would guess we'll probably only get there a week early.

CHAPTER 28

I have been offered things like baby duck, river eel, fish eyes, goat testicles and horse neck. I have a stomach of iron, and I don't know if it is from Grandma Ball or Grandpa Ray. Unlike my Mom and Dad, I can eat anything, but I am careful when I eat these things. At the end of a tournament all is fair game. I figure the worst thing that can happen is a long ride home, but during play, I never explore my taste buds.

The difficult part, and this is tricky, is not to offend whoever is with you, so I try to keep dinners with the locals to after the competitions. My first year in Japan, I had to explain to the president of our club that the night before a final is not the best time for me to try Sake for the first time. We lost, so maybe he knew something I didn't.

When I was playing in Japan, my parents came to visit Sarah and me. They always came to visit the places I played until my sisters started having families, and then their vacation time got used up fast. Anyway, we went out for dinner the first night they arrived and we went to a fish restaurant where we got a surprise. As we walked in, the chef was there at the door, and right away he asked us to pick what we wanted to eat out of a tank by the door. This tank belonged at Sea World. There were all types of fish, crabs, lobsters, octopus, etc. My Mom and Dad were like, Oh my God. Once we picked it out. They brought it to our table still flopping around so we could make sure it was fresh. It was so funny to see this squid, crab and red snapper flopping around the table, and 30 minutes later we were eating them. My Mom actually tried some stuff, like squid on a stick and fermented, pickled fish, but Dad was unwilling.

One Easter in Greece, we went to my coach's house in the country with the whole team. He had two huge spits going and each had a lamb roasting on it. I had never seen this before, but I can tell you, I ate half a lamb that day. It was the best meat I had ever eaten. Even Sarah, who is usually a little leery of meat products, admitted to liking it. Unfortunately, we had Ouzo to finish the meal, and it finished Sarah and me. We had to taxi home.

One year in Italy, Sarah and I took her parents to the restaurant of Pavarotti, the famous tenor. It was probably the best and most expensive meal I have ever had. We had fresh grilled rabbit, fresh ravioli with pumpkin, artichokes and Pana cotta for desert. We could have never gone, except out team's president set it up for us.

Needless to say, I have eaten some things that you can't find on a menu in Fort Wayne.

All in all, Sarah and I have had some interesting nights in Europe, like the first time we had visitors to our home in Russia. A teammate and his wife asked themselves over for dinner one night which was kind of forward, but normal for Russia. Sarah was worried about what to make, but then they called and said that they were bringing everything. Two hours later, they showed up with two hundred fresh mini shrimps and a case of Russian beer.

Well, my teammate's wife boiled them up in beer and lemon, and we peeled and ate for an hour. My son, Dyer, was the biggest fan, as he must have eaten 30. Whenever we went out to restaurants after that, he ordered boiled shrimp.

That reminds me of our second year in Greece. We had a day off, so we went to Halkidiki, a tourist spot on the sea. I had wanted to try this small fish Katsumura, a fish that is a little bigger than a sardine. They fry it all. They don't gut them at all, you just put it in your mouth and start chewing. I liked them, though they had a lot of flavor. Sarah was a no-go, but Dyer grabbed one and started in like they were potato chips, eating four or five. We took pictures of it. It was awesome, and I was so proud of him. Men eating disgusting stuff, there's nothing more macho than that.

I went to Italy with Sarah a year before I signed there in 2000. We wanted to check things out, and the team was trying to woo me so my agent, Pietro Peia, took us to this local meat restaurant. He knew I was a big meat eater, Midwest baby, so he recommended the steak Florentine. I was like, ok… I had no idea what it was, but I was in. Ten minutes later, Sarah and I hear this loud chopping noise coming from the kitchen, and he said that was my meat. I said, what? We went back, and here is the chef, with this enormous hatchet clobbering this half a side of beef. Fresh, huh? This steak was as big as I had ever seen, 22 ounces. They cooked it five minutes a side. We are talking, de-horn it, wipe its butt and send it in, rare. I loved it, the best steak I have ever eaten. I had always been a well-done steak guy (thanks, Dad) but after that I have ordered rare-to-medium rare every time.

CHAPTER 29

Team cultures are different in every country. In Russia and Italy, if a player has his birthday during the season he must bring in champagne and sweets for the team. This goes for a new baby and a new car as well. Needless to say, there is usually champagne and sweets every week.

In Japan, we would entertain ourselves on long trips by drawing on the young players with magic markers. Strange I know, but they would laugh for hours as we drew on their faces. Especially after a win, the team bus was full of young guys with glasses, mustaches and goatees drawn on their faces.

In Italy, I learned to dress for travel to and from games. With the USA team, we always wear our uniforms to the games and sweats after, but in Italy, they would show up to the games wearing Prada and Versace to the games. The guys were more like women. They wore more perfume than most women I know, and would take so much time on their bodies. We are talking waxing, tanning, lotion, etc. It was strange for a guy from the Midwest where a bar of soap was about all we needed, but they were very masculine and very confident, just pretty.

Team bus trips were always the most entertaining, and it's where I learned most of the different languages. Watching American films in another language will teach you in a hurry. I would always ask for English subtitles so that I could translate easier in my mind. Sometimes the movies were of the more sexually graphic in nature because in Greece, our team captain insisted in watching these before big matches. Needless to say the foreign players usually put their headphones on and laid down so they wouldn't see the screen.

Team saunas in Russia are very popular. In the United States, we tend not to spend much time naked around other men, but in Europe, men are very secure, and we have team sauna once a week, usually Mondays after a game on Sunday. Imagine 12 guys sitting in a room no bigger than most of our bathrooms, sweating out all the vodka they drank the night before, or the beer for the Americans. Then our massage guy comes in with a bunch of leaves tied together, and I don't know what kind of tree they come from. Anyway, a guy will lie down, covering important parts, and this guy will start smacking you with the leaves, and I mean smacking. He does both sides, then you get out and jump in a cold pool, and then run back in the sauna. It is supposed to open your pores and release the toxins from your body. Whatever it is, you feel great the next day.

Caffeine is a part of everybody's culture, but it is strange to me how different places put different importance on different types. America is a Starbucks Nation, big and milky. Japan is still a green tea culture, and any type of formal setting includes green tea. Canned coffee is also popular there, and you can get it cold or hot. Russia is a tea culture as well, but more the Earl Grey kind. They do drink coffee there, but tea after meals is more popular.

Italy is the coffee king. I always like coffee, but after Italy I was addicted. Coffee is my biggest vice, and I drink 10 cups a day. I bought an $800 espresso machine from Williams-Sonoma back home, just to get the Italian cafe kick. Cappuccino in the morning, never after noon, it's a rule. An espresso after every meal, or what the Italians just call café, and I throw a couple more in there for the heck of it.

Greece has its own take on coffee called a Frappe' which I don't see much in other places. It is a cold coffee, and they make it with instant coffee, milk, water and ice. It is blended and it is strong. They usually sip on it for two to three hours, adding water to it to make it last. Of course, we Americans drank them in 10 minutes and order another. They thought we were crazy. With Greece being warm most of the year, this drink was a great pick-me-up on a sunny afternoon.

CHAPTER 30

Not everybody can be a good professional club player because it is different than playing on national teams. National teams are organized. There is someone to take care of everything, to tell you what time to eat, sleep and go to the bathroom. They organize transportation, air travel, and visas.

Playing on a club is completely different. In most cases, it is up to the player to do everything. I have to get the visas to enter and work in these different countries, and that means dealing with consulates in the United States who are not the most cooperative people. They open for like two hours a day, they don't speak very good English and they are in no hurry to process your stuff.

I have to organize air travel for my family and then hope that the club pays me back for the tickets.

You have to be able to deal with the different cultures and different languages. Not all teams provide translators, so you better learn the language and learn it quickly, not only to function on the team but the clubs won't hesitate to quickly throw you on the radio and TV for interviews. My first year in Italy, after two weeks they put me on a TV program where they asked me what I thought about the women in Italy. My response was that I thought all the men here are beautiful. After that, I studied harder to learn the language.

You need to be strong mentally as well as physically. A team in Europe will cut you in a hurry or just not pay you if you don't perform, unlike the U.S. team which gives you a little leeway. The club teams don't care about you. If you stink, they will replace you. There are a lot of options for them, while the national team only has so many guys to pick from.

Another thing, pro teams reward individuals. I have always been a free spirit, prone not to listen all the time to those in authority. Ask my parents. I like the spotlight, I always have. Pro teams allow this and usually it lends itself to winning, where in a national team setting, it doesn't work as well. It has been a difficult thing to counterbalance the two. Pro ball has spectacular plays and players, national teams cultivate teamwork more.

Part of being a professional club player is dealing with the different languages. First, you have to decide if you want to learn them to be honest. If you have a one-year contract, do you really want to spend the time and effort to learn the language if you can get by without it? If it's someplace where you sign for longer, then it's probably something you need to invest some time in. It depends if it's a language you are interested in, like I think everyone in America should learn some kind of a Latin-based language, meaning French, Spanish or Italian. For one, it's easier for Americans to learn those languages because they are the most similar to ours with the same alphabet, sentence structure and sounds. In another 10 years, everyone here is going to speak Spanish anyway. Those you can learn hand in hand with each other. Spanish guys learn Italian in about three weeks. It's helpful.

In Italy, I knew I was going to be there a while so I wanted to learn. With Greece, I learned enough because I knew I was going to be there at least two years. I have no intention of learning Russian just because it's too hard, and I will never, ever speak it anywhere else. The same was true with Japanese, even though I was there for three years. It's a different alphabet and learning to write right to left and up and down. It was just not worth it in my opinion.

In all those languages I can say hello, how are you, my name is..., how have you been doing?... that kind of thing. Only in Italian can I actually have a meaningful conversation with people on something of substance. I can order in restaurants. I can say ``Waitress, can I have the soup please?" Obviously, it's not something you are going to get real far on, but it gets me by.

Sometimes it actually helps to be a volleyball player who plays overseas because we're pretty famous over there. In Russia, even though I've only been there a year in a half, if we go to Moscow, Kazan or St. Petersburg, people know who I am. It's the same in the North of Italy, too. If I go to Thessaloniki, the second biggest city in Greece, I get mobbed. I can't walk down the street without someone wanting to buy me a methos or giving me a hero or something. I haven't been back to Japan in six years, but when we went back there for the World Cup, we had fans waiting in the lobby every day from 6 a.m. to 6 p.m. That doesn't happen too much here.

When we played for the club team in Iraklis, there were 10,000 people there for the finals. There were 8,000 people at the Russian Cup finals. We're on big-screen jumbotrons, we're on commercials for BMWs, Any time we go to a restaurant or a bar, we don't pay for anything. I think I get charged double here in Fort Wayne sometimes.

Not being recognized at first was a little bit upsetting as a young athlete who thinks you're pretty good. In Fort Wayne obviously I'm recognized because volleyball is sort of important there, but other places in American not so much. Maybe in Southern California a little bit, but in Italy there's a paper just for volleyball. In Russia, the Sports Express has three pages on volleyball. How many pages of any book or magazine in America is on volleyball? It's just a different lifestyle.

Before I was a little bitter about it, but now it's nice to have two different lives and I enjoy coming back here. I'm not sure I'd want to be that well known seeing how Brian Cardinal and Brad Miller and those guys have to deal with fame here. Americans aren't very nice. If you lose, they are throwing rocks at your house. If you went to Purdue and they are for IU, they are driving by and giving you the finger. In Europe they are appreciative, win or lose, for the work you do for them and their team. They want you to win, but besides some of the soccer hooligans which is a separate thing, fans for volleyball and basketball are great in Europe. They don't sit on their hands like they do here. They clap win or lose, they cheer, they sing, they dance, they come to the airport at 4 a.m. to celebrate when you win. It's good.

Then when I come home I can just have a normal life again.

CHAPTER 31

They've been less and less over the years, but I always find myself, especially if we start winning something, always going back with my superstitions, even on the national team. None of this makes a bit of difference except in my own head. There are so many little ones that I don't even think about them.

Sometimes after practices or games, my mom always gave me a hard time about turning your socks the right way. If we're winning, no matter how the socks come back, inside or outside, that's how I wear them. If one didn't get washed, if one stinks or has blood on it, it's going right back on the same foot.

People always say you put your pants on one leg at a time, but I have to put my left shoe on first. Sometimes I'll be talking and I'll put my right shoe on first, and I'll realize it and take my shoes off, take my socks off and start all over again. The left one has to go on first, and I can't tell you why. Even if we lose, I stick with that one.

Whatever song I listened to last before we go out on the court, if we win, before the next game, I have to listen to the same song right before we go out.

Whatever meal we have before a match, usually chicken or beef, if we win I have the exact same meal the next day.

I always drink a Red Bull before every match. I've made people run across the street to supermarkets to get one because I have to have one before every game.

I painted my toenails before my first Olympics and thank goodness that one wore off. My crazy wife, I let her paint my toenails one time in 1996, and we started off real hot so I kept it going. All of a sudden I realized the abuse I was taking from my teammates and it wasn't worth it. I'd almost rather lose than take that abuse any more.

I always sit in the same spot if we go somewhere I've played before and won. I'll make people get out of the position I sat in last time. In hotel rooms, no matter who I stay with, I always have to have the bed closest to the bathroom. That's for a lot of reasons.

I never wear my game jersey outside or leave it untucked. Nowadays guys show up to matches already wearing their uniforms or their game shoes. Ever since I was little, I was told you don't wear your game shoes outside, and I still don't. I wear sandals or different shoes until we get there and then I'll put my game shoes on. They can't touch outside.

I'm also one of the few guys who warms up in a T-shirt and then changes into my uniform. Everyone else starts in their uniforms, but I don't like getting my uniform sweaty before I actually start playing the game so just before as the game starts, I'll change out of my T-shirt and put my uniform on. Now there's all kind of rules that you can't do that in front of people, and you have to leave the court so I'll leave the court and do that. When I put the shirt on, that means I'm ready. I don't want it all sweaty and nasty before I start, and I've been that way since college.

I guess that's a lot, but it's funny because I'll feel it if something is out of whack, and, if we lose, I'll change things up. I won't change putting my left shoe on first, but I'll switch the food or the songs. It's just feeling comfortable. Sometimes I'll remember that I didn't sit in the same place or whatever and I'll start warming up and I will actually think about it, like I feel bad. It will bother me and then somebody will ask what I'm thinking about and then I'll try to forget about it and get it out of my head. It's just so stupid.

In my sport and my job, as the pressure increases, as the stress of winning and losing, which often comes with trophies, money and medals – with all that stuff you want to make sure you leave no stone unturned if you think it can help you. I've been in games where I start warming up, and I'll think, ``You know what, I put my right shoe on first." Then I'll go back to the locker room, take them off and put them on again.

I probably would have forgotten about it, but it bothered me as I was warming up for a big game, so instead of letting it bother me, I just go change it and move on.

A lot of times it's been a forced thing. Maybe we've traveled and we're playing a team in Champions' League where we know we're going to win, maybe I forgot that my socks weren't turned the right way. Maybe I was in a hurry because the plane was late or the bus was late so I just did it. Of course the whole game I'm thinking about it, but it didn't matter because we weren't playing anybody who was any good. If it was an important game or it was somebody who was pretty good, I probably would have sent somebody out to buy what I needed or I would have made sure I was content with my set up for the game.

CHAPTER 32

I've been real lucky with most of the coaches I've had. They haven't been anywhere near the same as far as personality. Each guy has had his own different style, going all the way back to junior high. Don Wickman at Central Lutheran grade school in New Haven was the Lord's right hand in football and basketball coaches. I always reacted well to fear, not that my dad was that big hand at home. We were afraid of him, but that's how parenting was. I'm kind of the same, the whole, ``I'm not your friend, I'm your father, and I'm teaching you right and wrong." Coaches were the same way. I'm not your friend, I'm here to teach you how to play this game and play it correctly with the right ethics. Now today it's all ``Let's all feel good about each other." I still remember with coach Wickman the dirty dozen, the 12 defensive drills we had to do until our little seventh grade legs wouldn't run any more on that concrete gym floor. He really instilled the kind of ferocity that I had as a young athlete. Then I went to Woodlan where Gay Martin was the exact opposite and it was a privilege to play varsity as a freshman. He didn't really push me so much as allow me to develop on my own. Then I had the freedom to play outside and to run up and down the court, and that really allowed me to train a lot on my own. Don kind of pushed me and then I had to learn to push myself a little bit.

As far as the national team, Bill Neville was my first influence on the international level with his old school way letting you grovel and die and lose until you figured it out for yourself. Instead of calling a time out when you were down 8-0, he was going to make the team figure it out. You may lose 15-0 or you were going to come back, and, as he would say, you were going to pull yourself up by your bootstraps and grind it out and get back in the game. He made people build their character instead of just giving players the answers the way coaches like to do now. As a coach you instruct your players, but there's something to coaches who make players learn things on their own, especially when he knew they had that in them. He knew I could figure out problems and grow from that. I think I struggled emotionally. I would get mad and angry and lash out, but eventually I would figure it out. Coach Neville was the first coach, more so than my dad, who understood my psychology as a young athlete. I didn't understand it. I was on an emotional rollercoaster half the time, but I think he saw the potential not only physically but mentally for me to develop into a strong volleyball player, which I believe I am now. But it took me a long time to get there. It wasn't something at 24 or 28 I figured out, maybe at 30 and at 36 I'm still figuring it out. I attribute a lot of the psychology of the game to Bill and learning how to win under all kinds of circumstances.

I owe a lot to Rick Butler. Back in college when I was struggling with weight, and struggling in the summers with not playing on the national team because of Canyon Ceman or Mike Sealy. He basically took me aside one day and said, ``Look, you're not going to be better than these guys unless you get off your you-know-what and train and lose some weight and put down the beer and get serious about what you do. If you don't want to do that, that's fine, but quit wasting my time and USA Volleyball's time by saying you want to do this when obviously you don't because of your actions." That's not something anyone had said to me before, and luckily I took the challenge and dropped 25 pounds and got serious about my game. I finished off my college career well and went right to the national team. I wouldn't say I'm a fitness freak, but I've always been away of what I needed to do when it came to diet and training and whatever to make sure I can play at the level I need to play at. Before, because I was young, I could stay up all night and maybe have one too many and still be better than everybody else because I was better than everybody else at that time. Then all of a sudden everybody is 20-something and they're all that good and that wasn't going to get it done anymore. Luckily, Rick taught me that and I owe the turnaround in my career to him.

When I went to the national team, I started out full-time with Fred Sturm. I can't really say he taught me anything. I don't think he's a bad coach, just more analytical than anybody I've ever had. He was more of a stat guy, a numbers guy than other coaches I had who were more motivational or more technical. We didn't have any problems, but I can't say I enjoyed playing under him so much. I didn't loathe him, either, it was just kind of a time in my life.

Then I played for Doug Beal most of the time in my USA career. Doug is a hard read. I still don't know how he feels about me after about 10 years together. I guess respect is the first word when I think about Doug because you have to because of all the time and energy he's put into USA Volleyball, even though sometimes I think some of the stuff he wants to do is unproductive. I still can't shortchange the man for the time and effort he has put in. Second, anybody who has won a gold medal as a player or a coach you have to respect. Thirdly, I actually respect the candor he has. He's pretty much a straight shooter as far as he's not going to blow wind up your skirt, or if you stink he's going to tell you you stink or if you're not going to play he's going to tell you. There isn't a lot of gray area, which I think is good in a coach. After that, he was the head coach so he always wanted to be in charge, but so did I as the setter. I'm a firm believer that once a game starts, the coach's roll is pretty much done. There are some strategic time outs or substitutions but anybody can do that. I think a coach makes his team in training. That's where he earns his money, and once a game starts, if the team isn't ready, you've already blown it as a coach. Then it's up to the players on what they have from what you've taught them or what they have inside, those things that make or break the game. He and I butted heads because once the whistle blew, I wanted it to be my team and sometimes I would do things he didn't agree with, but as the guy on the court in the spur of the moment I felt I was doing the right things to help the team win. He didn't always see it that way and that's when our conflicts would come and go. I would like to think at the end of the Olympics in Athens that we left each other with mutual respect. He knows I put a lot of blood, sweat and tears into the USA red, white and blue, and I know he has done the same. We were never going to be good friends because our personalities are completely different. I've heard the man tell a joke and everyone just sat there because he's not funny, and he thinks he's is. He's intelligent and he's clever, but he's one of those dry sense of humor guys and I'm more a slapstick guy and you couldn't pick two guys further apart on the spectrum of what men are supposed to be. Our teamwork together could have been more successful, but it wasn't too bad, and he kept playing me so I must not have been too bad of a guy, and I didn't quit so he must not have been too bad.

Hugh McCutcheon is like the new breed of coaching. It's strange because we actually played against each other when he was at BYU and we're about the same age. He's a little more the new breed of touchy, feely, sensitive and everyone's inner child needs something, which I'm not a big fan of. I came back to the team and we had psychologists there talking about getting into the zone and how to step into the now, and I'm rolling my eyes and shaking my head thinking, are you kidding me. I let him know that I thought that was baloney. If you need that kind of help to get ready for a big game or to train for the Olympics, then you should do something else. Unfortunately, now we have some guys on the team who are always looking for the answers. ``Why did I make that mistake?" You just did. The best thing about my game the last five years and a guy named Sean Rooney who's going to be real good for us, is that sometimes you just have to say, ``Whatever." I made a bad set. ``Whatever." It happens. You're going to shank a ball or serve it into the net, it's the sport. There are always mistakes, but guys who are always ``Why did I serve that poorly? Was my arm too low? Was my footwork correct? Should my toss be higher?" Then you are just going to over-think it. Sometimes you can do everything right and it still doesn't work. Sometimes people ask me why we lost, and maybe we played great, but they played better. It's sports. That's why people watch and cheer for underdogs. There are no guarantees. So Hugh is a little too mental training for me.

He is very knowledgeable about the game and he has a nice balance of the tactical, analytical side as well as the physical, emotional, rah-rah side, so he has a nice mixture of the two together. For me the only thing is, I'd like to see him a little less emotionally involved with the guys and just do everything else he does. I think he's a good guy to lead us into these Olympics.

CHAPTER 33

A relationship between a father and a son comes in all different shapes and sizes. Some fathers and sons don't get along because they are constantly banging heads. Some sons are so different from their fathers, that it is difficult to have a meaningful relationship with each other. Some fathers and sons are so much alike that they can't share the same space with each other because it always feels like there isn't enough room. And some fathers and sons just love each other and support each other no matter what their personal characteristics are.

I guess it was Sarah, my wife, who first noticed the similarities between my father and I: How I smiled crooked for pictures, how I loved an audience, how I crossed my legs at the kitchen table while talking and how his hairline had found my head. Lloy Ball was becoming Arnie Ball. If I wasn't already.

Let me start by saying that most of my good qualities come from my Mom and her side of the family. She was the one who got us all out of bed on Sundays for church. She made sure we visited grandparents on weekends, and she was the one who made sure all work was done before TV could be watched. My Mom doesn't get near enough mention in our family. But anyone who really knows our clan knows that Sandy is the glue that holds us all together. She is the best mother any child could ever ask for. And luckily, Sarah is taking right after her.

Back to Armond. After watching him for basically my whole childhood, it is no wonder that I took on so many of his traits. I remember him ranting and raving during his younger days at the kids at Harding High School. I remember him being the only Dad who could ever really do anything athletic because he was always in great shape. I remember how competitive he was on and off the court. My Mom wouldn't even play cards with him because he had to win. He was the only guy on his 50 and younger team at nationals that would still dive on the floor after balls.

I remember playing one-on-one outside in the cold at our Woodburn house. Especially as I got bigger, I would try to back him into the paint, and he would punch me in the back to keep me out. Then, one day when I think I was 16, I turned and dunked on him. That was the end of one-on-one. After that he would only play H-O-R-S-E. If he couldn't win, he didn't want to play.

I believe that competitiveness rubbed off on me, more later in life, when I had to really fight for things. I always tell people when they ask me why I train every day, especially at my age, I say that right now somewhere there is a young setter training his butt off to beat me out of my position, and I am not ready to give it up.

My dad has always helped me with sports, but not like most people think. He was never the pushy, loud, over-beating dad like you see everywhere nowadays. He would help if other dads wanted him to coach, and he would practice with me, but only when I asked. He never told me what or when to play. He only told me these two things, and I tell them to Dyer already today. 1. If you start something, you finish it. Some kids would come out for a sport and not like it or find out it was too hard, and their parents would let them quit. Not my dad. If I signed up, I was in it to the end. 2. If you're going to play, play 100 percent. If not, don't waste the team's time. Two easy and simple rules that I think everybody should follow.

My dad didn't get to see me play that much in high school. My basketball season and his volleyball season were at the same time so he made it to as many games as he could. Sometimes he would make his team come and it was always so funny. They would sit in the Woodlan student body section and hold up newspapers when the other team was announced and do crazy cheers just for me. I really liked it because, like I have mentioned before, I wasn't really liked that much in high school. I know that to this day Dad wishes he could have seen me play more. That goes for now, too. I have been so many places and won so many things, and he has tried to get to as many of them as possible, but I know he would like to watch me play more. I always get in the DVDs of our World Cup or Russian championship matches. Mom says he stays up late at night and watches them.

This is going to sound weird, but I think all of that is a big part of me. I play for him. Now as I have gotten older, I of course play to support my family. I play because I love to play, but a big part of me plays for him. To make him proud, I am still his boy. And I have always appreciated the patience he showed towards me during my sports career, especially during my IPFW days. To say that I got occasionally distracted would be an understatement. Not too many other fathers would have done the same. I play for him because if he had my size and ability, I know he would have been great. I play for that look. It is a look that he doesn't give just anybody. His wife, children and grandchildren may get it sometimes, but it is the look of approval. And anyone who has been in my father's life knows this look. It doesn't happen often, but when it does you'll never forget, and you'll do what ever it takes to see it again.

Lastly, my father is my hero. Young kids at schools and reporters always ask me who inspired you, who is your hero? And I always say my father. Once again, not because my Mom or Sarah or anyone else is less important to me. I love them all in different types of relationships. But, like I mentioned at the beginning, fathers and sons have different bonds. The best way I can describe mine with Dad is that I want to be just like him, if I'm not already. And I hope someday Dyer will say the same thing about me.

CHAPTER 34

This may shock some people, but I don't want my son Dyer to play volleyball. It is a dying sport, and I don't think he will have the opportunities I did when he gets older. That might surprise people, but I don't want him to have to struggle to find places to play like Dad and I did when we were growing up.

I hope he plays football, baseball or basketball, but I would be even happier if he is very intelligent and is a doctor or scientist.

I honestly believe that because volleyball is a dying sport. That's not an easy thing for me to say out loud, especially knowing all the time and effort that my father has put into the sport and knowing all the work and time I have put into the sport. Despite knowing all the life experiences and financial security the sport has given me, I would still not want my son to play the sport.

Men's volleyball has gone nowhere for going on 30 years. I know this because the United States has won two Olympic gold medals (in 1984 and 1988) and a bronze medal (in 1992), and there's still no professional league in this country. Give me any other country that wouldn't have made those results into a gold mine.

The big problem is this: People love to play volleyball, in their backyards, in the pool and in recreation leagues, but when it comes to paying to watch it, forget it. It's just not a sport that fits into our culture. There is no contact, there are no spectacular plays, slam dunks, home runs or hole-in-ones, and it is difficult to understand.

No matter what we do or the success we've had on the men's national team, it has been and will always be seen as a chicks' sport! Despite having said that, I would love for my daughter Mya to play volleyball. Why? Two words, Title IX. Women's college teams have 13 scholarships, and there are over 400 schools to choose from. That's a free education. It's not quite the same for men where there are around 60 schools splitting up 4.5 scholarships each. It's a sport that always seems to be fighting to survive, and it can never grow because of Title IX.

I have given up. I am going to try to get my medal, and keep making my money, but, as far as things I can do or anyone else can do to help our sport, there is nothing. I've seen my father fight this fight for his entire life and there have been no improvements.

Here's one more example: The move of the U.S. teams of their training facilities from Colorado Springs to Anaheim is a joke! The only good thing about the move is that younger players are more accessible. Besides that, we still draw the same lousy crowds, and this is in what is supposedly the Mecca of volleyball, Southern California. All that means is the players have even more distractions than before, and financially it is even harder to support the team there where it has to compete against everything else for corporate and fan support and media attention.

When we were in Colorado Springs, we were one of the biggest things in town. That's something this sport can't afford to ever take for granted.

Ever since I was big enough to think about it, playing professional volleyball was my real dream. Sure, there were moments that the NBA crept in my mind, but I never really thought of myself as a basketball player until the end of my high school days. I remember watching our men's volleyball team win the gold medal in 1984. My Dad and I watched that game over and over again, and when I heard that guys like Karch Kiralry and Steve Timmons were making $500,000 to $1 million in Italy, well that was that. I wanted to do what they did.

Of course, I didn't realize how difficult playing professionally and winning a gold medal were to do. One I have accomplished, the other has not happened yet, and the days of that possibility are fading.

Those dreams will not be real by the time Dyer is old enough to play for several reasons. USA Volleyball has been unable to start and sustain a pro league, the number of men's college teams continues to dwindle and in my opinion the international leagues will slowly decrease their salaries in the future. Playing pro volleyball isn't a viable option for my son in the future.

Plus, living overseas isn't the great life that most of my friends and family think it is. It's not like I am over here sightseeing, shopping in Milan, drinking coffee in Paris and climbing Mt. Fuji. I am actually working. Granted, it's not your typical 9-to-5 that most Midwest people work, but what I do in four hours every day is more physically demanding than most people do in a month. And besides hotels and gyms, I don't see much of Europe.

So, having said this, I want my son to really think about this life if he is considering volleyball as a career.

Another point is that I don't feel a young USA player can get the kind of training to be successful in the pro leagues. Only recently have players from the U.S. cracked into the good leagues and the good contracts, and most of these players are older who have paid their dues and learned the international game overseas.

Having my Dad as a coach, I will be careful how I put this: There are few coaches qualified to teach players the international game. I am not saying there are not good coaches, there are; but these coaches only know how to teach U.S. methods and ideologies of play, most of the Doug Beal school of volleyball, using techniques that were good in the 1980s but that doesn't translate to the game or players of today.

I think there are a few exceptions. Even though I have never played for UCLA coach Al Scates, he seems to understand how to make players win and gives them an inner confidence that flows well with overseas play. If you are not confident in Italy, Russia, Greece..... they will eat you alive. I think UC-Irvine coach John Speraw will be one of these coaches. He is a new breed of coach that can technically teach kids how to play the game correctly.

And, of course, my Dad, whom I have always held in the highest respect as a coach. To do what he has done in a city like Fort Wayne is a miracle. There's no high school volleyball, it's not an easy city to lure players to and the weather is typical upper Midwest in the winter, but every year he has team that not only clobbers big-time schools like Ball State, Ohio State and Penn State but he goes and vies for the national championship. He is the most underrated coach in the nation. Finally, in 2007, the American Volleyball Coaches Association figured it out and awarded him the coach of the year.

For all of those reasons I don't want Dyer to play volleyball. Saying that, if 10-year old Dyer comes to me and says, "Dad. I want to play volleyball," I'll remember all the things I've talked about above, and then I will do everything in my power to find him a place to play even if it means I set up a club for him just as my Dad did.

CHAPTER 35

I've spent the last year preparing for my fourth and last Olympics.

It was one of the hardest decisions that I have ever made. The amount of time and energy that goes into playing with the National Team is much more than most people understand. Some of the things I had to consider were four-to-six hours physical work every day, terrible flights and long travel, and most of all being away from family and friends. It also meant I had to live most of this year away from Sarah and the kids.

I thought I was finished with USA Volleyball following Athens, but Coach Hugh McCutcheon called me last December after the team had a terrible World Championships. He asked me if I was interested in considering a return to the team. I told him my family and I would talk about it and I would let him know after the Russian season. Hugh was a good salesman, telling me everything I wanted to hear, about how good I am, how the team needs me, and the other players are better now. Looking back, I probably should have played harder to get.

There was an awful lot that had to go into making this decision on a couple of different fronts. Sarah and I first had to decide if we were going to play for the national team again, and if we were going to do that, if we were going to play in Russia again. Playing in Russia was OK, but playing for the national team again meant being gone all year because I'd be training or playing with them whenever I wasn't in Russia. Maybe it's OK if you go back to Russia by yourself if you're going to be home with the family all summer in Fort Wayne, but then we decided to do both which meant all summer I was in Anaheim.

The big part of it was we really didn't have a choice in taking the family back to Russia because there is no school over there, and Dyer had to go to school, so they had to stay here. If I'm going to be in the Olympics, then I need to continue to play in Russia, plus the money is so good that we have to do it. Sarah was the first one to say that even if they had come with me to Russia, with my travel schedule back and forth for World Cup, Champions League and different tournaments, they wouldn't have seen me that much anyway, plus it's cold there and you can't take the kids outside and the food is not that great. So we decided they would stay in Fort Wayne this year.

Sarah was a big factor in my return to the USA team as well. Usually she doesn't say much about my career stuff, and that is the great thing about my wife. We do not talk volleyball, and I think that is one reason why we have been together and happy so long because my life outside volleyball is real normal. She really doesn't care about me as a player but as a man, and in this case, she decided to give me her opinion. She told me that this would absolutely be the last time they asked me to play, and that I was playing great, and that she and Dyer would come to China to see me. Then, thinking about Sarah, Dyer and my Mom and Dad watching me play in the Olympics really got my blood pumping. As an athlete, we are given a short window to do our thing, and then we are forgotten. If I can still help a team win, which I can, she told me to go for it, so I did.

I'm playing for a few reasons: I am still the best setter in the United States and maybe the world, the U.S. team won't ask me again, nor will I physically be able to. I want my son, wife, mom, dad and sisters to see me one more time in the red, white and blue.

I guess in the end I feel like a have more to give. I feel like I haven't played as well as I can in that event, and while I have the ability and desire to still do it, it would be a disservice to myself not to go again. People don't have a clue how badly I want to win, but one thing I have learned in my 13 years of playing is that I can't do it alone. I have tried, but without quality players around me, winning the big matches isn't possible.

Even though I'm 36, I decided to play because over the past years I have shown that I am getting better with age. Of course the jumping and quickness aren't as good, but the skills and intelligence gets better. I think my game is just more refined, the quality of my sets is better. Another important factor is I don't feel pressure from coaches or the situations to play a certain way, I do what I know works and what I do best. I stay aggressive where before I would pull back in tight spots. The biggest thing is my mentality. I am not afraid to lose. I don't go crazy too much any more, I stay within my own game and let the things around me happen.

I feel like I am playing the best ball of my life, but, I also know it will end soon, so I am going to ride this bull till it bucks me. I don't do near the training I used to, I pace myself to ensure that I am healthy for the matches. At this point in my career I don't need more reps, just stay in shape and play the games.

I think we proved that when we qualified for the Olympics by winning the NORCECA tournament in Puerto Rico in January. We won all five matches without losing a set. Now that we've qualified, I'm going to eat and sleep well and really try to get fit. I will use the last few months in Russia to train and lose a few pounds so I can have three weeks at home after the Russian Championships to rest and just keep my form before I go back to the National Team.

As for this Olympic team, this team is a lot like other teams I have played on. We have the capability to be real good a lot of times, but we also have a tendency to let our level drop off and lose concentration sometimes. It's frustrating. Just like in the World Cup, we beat Brazil and Bulgaria and go five with Russia, and then lose to Puerto Rico and Spain. Some of the guys just don't understand that some days as a player you will not feel good, fresh or in the zone, but you still have to have a good level of play. There are always things that a player can do to help the team when he doesn't have his ``A" game. It is a question of being selfish, and becoming a role player when you can't be the man you think you are that day.

I don't know what makes a veteran. I used to think it was time on the team, but we have a lot of guys who have played a long time who don't act like veterans. A vet to me is someone who has been in meaningful matches, not playing Japan 100 times, but playing in Italian, Greek, French, Russian and European Cup finals and of course World Cups, World Championships and Olympic matches. Those are the ones that make you into a better player, once it's all on the line, and a team needs an important play, not a spectacular play, but just good volleyball. We have some guys that can do that, but not enough. I hope that this past World Cup has taught some of our guys that.

To be honest, I don't really work with the younger setters much, not because I don't want to, but I didn't like when older guys told me what to do. If they ask, I happily give them advice, but it is a tough situation. I am replacing a guy who waited for me to quit so he could have the position, and then I came back and he was less than happy. Once a few years ago, he actually asked me not to come back so he could have a chance. I lost respect for him after that. The younger setters will figure things out as they go. I did. Being so much older than them makes it difficult to be real close. Now, I understand how Jeff Stork must have felt about me when he came back and I was there. Fitting into a pre-existing group is tough, especially when there are guys who are 10 years younger than me. That is just nuts. They go out every night, they have energy all the time and they are living a life that has no responsibilities, the same way I did 10 years ago.

My approach to this Olympics is totally different because I will enjoy it. If we don't win I will not be devastated. That doesn't mean I don't want to win, or I won't do everything possible to win, but I have learned that the next day is going to come either way. So, I won't play not to lose, and I'll leave everything out on the court for my team and then move on. This has really helped me deal with all the stuff that is involved with the national team. I think we can win, otherwise I wouldn't play, but I am not going to put any pressure on myself like I did in the past. I am going to play ball, enjoy my teammates and enjoy China with my family. I won't make any predictions.

I won't be the captain this time, and I love that. While it was a great honor, I am already the leader on the court whether I have the bar under my number or not. The added responsibilities like press conferences, extra meetings and so on are just too much. Tom Hoff can have it.

I can actually say I will be relieved when it is over. Not in a bad way, but to know that this chapter of my life is done will finally give me some closure and I'll be able to move on to the next phase of my life. There won't be any tears. After China, I will never wear a USA jersey again, unless there's an oldtimer's game.

CHAPTER 36

In a lot of ways this has been the hardest year of my career, and let me give you a little taste of what it's been like. This is the first time I have been alone the entire time while playing, but there were good reasons for that. When I am with the National Team, I am alone because our home is Fort Wayne, and Dyer is in school and it's not fair to drag him, Mya and Sarah out to California, especially since I am rarely there. The USA team travels so much, and it is sometimes weeks at a time so I wouldn't be there anyway and they would be in a strange place without me and without family and friends.

Then in Kazan, my city in Russia, there isn't an International school, meaning no school where English is the primary language. It's not fair to Dyer to try and have him learn Russian for one year, and then when we go back to the States he would be behind the other kids. So, I am alone in Russia. I have played pro ball for 11 years and this is the first time I've gone solo, and it sucks. Not only am I getting beat up physically by playing on two teams, I am mentally stressed, worried about my family all the time. I call twice a day to talk to Sarah and the kids, but because of the love that we have for each other, and the fact that I can't make this kind of living back in the States, we sacrifice this year for the betterment of our lives. At least that is what I tell myself.

I spend about $1,500 a week on my cell phone bill, and sometimes I call twice a day. I love to text and so does Sarah so we communicate a lot that way. At the end of my day, her morning, I'll call, and she'll tell me what happened the whole day. I talk to Dyer almost every day, and then Mya will steal the phone and yab at me and then eventually hang up on me.

With the internet, Sarah sends me pictures all the time. We make due, and every time I came back from the national team, I've always been able to stop in at home for a couple days. As long as they keep hearing my voice and seeing my face, they know that I love them.

Whenever I have free time in Russia, basically I'm either in two positions. I'm either sleeping in the bed or I'm laying down on the couch with the internet next to me on a chair and I'm watching NBA Television. I was lucky enough to get a satellite with all the sports packages back here. I have a DSL line for the internet. Clay Stanley is there without his girlfriend so we usually go to dinner every night and then the rest of the time I just hang out at the house. There's not too much exciting to do, but we play every three or four days so we're pretty busy.

I'm trying to stay focused on my goal, but being alone for Christmas was very hard. I watched my kids open their gifts from Santa through the internet, and I got to look at photos that Sarah sent me after the fact. I missed New Year's also because the national team coach made us train in Los Angeles before we went to Puerto Rico for the Olympic Qualifier, which is fine to the other guys because they all live there, but I am the only one who has his family elsewhere.

To people who think I don't suffer and sacrifice to trying reach my dreams and financially take care of my family, well, think again. Is it all worth it? I hope to God it is. I do know this, those who chose not to strive, fight and realize their dreams are the ones who lose out. I only get one life, and I will do everything possible to make sure I don't waste it such as seeing the faces on my kids when I can give them things I never had, when we move into our new house and when my son sits in the stands in China and watches his Dad play for the USA. That's when I will know it is all worth it.

CHAPTER 37

Looking at the end of my career and the rest of my life, I have about a dozen things I would like to do, but none are set 100 percent. And no, coaching isn't really one of them – well, maybe later on.

I plan on taking two years and doing nothing. I will enjoy being a U.S. citizen, and enjoy being a husband and father. Then, I would like to open a sports bar in Angola, a small town about 50 miles North of Fort Wayne where we are building our dream house. I would have my sister Amy and her husband Jamie move back and join my cousin Steve to help me run it. Or I will open a home design business for my wife because Sarah has the best taste in the world, and could decorate anyone's home or business. Or I will continue with a small business I have now. A few friends and I buy older or broken down homes and fix them up, then we rent them or sell them depending on what the market is doing. The market being as it is lately, this idea may end quickly. Or I would like to work for my friend who works in NASCAR. He and I have spoken about me being a contract closer for them. Basically, I would get to schmooze and socialize with bigwigs and make sure they sign the contracts that NASCAR and they agreed on. Sounds like fun.

In the past I've had an interest in television, and I studied communications in college. I don't think it's something I'm going to pursue, but it's something I would entertain if someone ever came to me. If I ever crossed paths with someone at ESPN or Fox, and they wanted me to do volleyball or local basketball, I'd consider it. I think I would enjoy it, and I think I have the skills for it, but it would be a part-time thing. I don't want anything where I have to be gone every night away from my family. I've already done that.

I've also thought a little bit in the past about possibly coaching, but that's not in my top 10, and I get a little tired about people asking me about it all the time. I can't say that it's never going to happen, but it's last on my list. It just looks real hard. I can't really say it any plainer than that. I'm not a huge fan of women's sports and nor do I want to coach them. I think men's volleyball is a dying sport in this country, and the time commitment of trying to talk young, 18-year-old guys into coming to play for you, more travel, coaching guys like me. The more I thought of it, the less attractive it became. People assume that every player will be a coach when he retires. The fact is, good players really don't make good coaches, except my Dad of course. Most coaches were decent players but not stars. Stars don't know how to coach people how to do things. They always just did it. They don't know why or how.

I also see the emotional roller coaster my dad goes on. I've had that. I've felt that way in my job for the last 15 years. When my team loses, I'm so emotionally down. When my team wins, I'm so emotionally high. I really don't wan to continue that roller coaster. Thank God, Sarah, after 15 years, knows when to talk to me and when not to talk to me. When we come home, we talk about the business side of volleyball, but we never talk about the game or how I play or anybody else on the team. She knows I think of that enough on my own so it's nice to have the distraction or normalcy that she brings.

I'm not 100 percent sure what I'm going to do with the rest of my life, but I know one thing for sure. I'm going to have fun trying to be the best husband and father I can possibly be.

CHAPTER 38

Looking back and thinking about this summer, we had our two biggest events in volleyball, the World League and then the summer Olympics in Beijing. For those who don't know, the World League is made up of the very best teams in the world playing home and home matches throughout the spring and summer, with the final six teams meeting in the tournament finals, this time in Brazil.

Because it was an Olympic year, all the teams approached the World League a little differently this year, saying, "It's not that important to win, you have to play certain guys, rest certain guys," which was all kind of smoke and mirrors because everyone wants to win it. The players all want to win it because it's a big event and it pays about three times what the gold medal pays. Plus, you get the chance to play teams you're going to play in the Olympics and stay sharp.

The ironic thing about it is we were real close to not being in the final four of the event. We get bageled by Serbia out of the gate and then had to scratch and claw to win a five-game series from Poland. Then it was still up to Serbia to beat Poland for us to get into the semifinals. If Poland had won that match, we'd have been going home early, and Poland would have gone to the semifinals against Brazil. Think about this… in my opinion that semifinal game against Brazil started this whole chain reaction for what we later accomplished, and here we were at the mercy of the Polish team. Had they had a better effort against Serbia, for sure we don't win the World League and then maybe we don't have the confidence that we took into Beijing.

In a big tournament you have to have health, timing and luck. I don't think we were lucky during the Olympics, but that little bit of luck was as important as anything else to propel us to where we ended up going.

By that time, we had been together for about six weeks training and playing in the World League, but coach McCutcheon made a pretty big decision the week before the finals. Because we had done so well earlier, we were guaranteed a spot in the final six in Rio, but we had one last trip for the regular season to Varna, Bulgaria. No offense to the Bulgarians, that's not exactly a great place to go a couple of days before we would have had to be in Rio to play. We would have had to fly from L.A. to Bulgaria and then right to Rio. Hugh made the call of keeping the four older guys – me, Reid Priddy, Tom Hoff and Ryan Millar – back in Anaheim so we could rest and train. Then we'd meet them in Rio, so it was planning for the long haul. It didn't exactly help our chances as soon as we got down there because there was a hurricane happening in Florida so the four of us got delayed and only got in about 18 hours before we had to play. That's why we got the beatdown against Serbia, losing 3-0.

We then had to turn around and play Poland the next day, and they got up 2-1. We won the fourth game, though they had a swing at match point. They led 24-23 when the ball hit off Reid's head, Riley Salmon chased it down in middle back, I had to bump set Clay Stanley and he hit a kill. Then we won the next two points. As much as I'd like to call that great volleyball skill, there was a lot of luck in that. The ball could have gone off his head and into the crowd. Two plays later we still had a chance to advance to the semis against Brazil.

Even after we won that match, most of us thought we were still done because Poland would beat Serbia. We were OK with that because we'd have a couple of extra days to go home to L.A., train, say goodbye to the family and then take off. Let me tell you though, once Poland lost to Serbia, there was a lot of whooping and hollering at the hotel because we wanted to play Brazil and we got a second boost of energy right then.

In the last couple of years we don't get real nervous playing Brazil, even though they are No. 1. We know they are team that usually steamrolls because they have more emotion than everybody else. It was 10 a.m.

and they had 11,000 people there to watch them, but we came out real intense. People get embarrassed by Brazil because they run a pipe and Giba or Dante will just hit it straight down or they run some crazy play and they bounce the ball up into the stands. All of a sudden they run off a couple more points because the other team is like, ``I can't believe that just happened." We've come to realize that an awesome play that brings the crowd to its feet is the same as a missed serve in the reality of it. We don't allow all the flying around and the craziness to affect us the way other teams do. We're not impressed. Our point doesn't look as pretty, but it's still 1-1. That's the mentality a lot of other teams don't take against them, and it gets them in trouble.

This has been Brazil's era, and even more than the fact that they have better players or better systems, there's a fear. The Bulls had it, the Pistons had it and the Colts had it the year they won. It's the overpowering sensation they apply to their opponents that you have no chance. It's how the Chinese felt at 10 a.m. when we played them in the Olympics. We walked out next to these boys, and here we are these men from the USA and you could see in their eyes, "This is going to be real quick because we have no business being on the court with these guys." We just don't let that affect us like other teams do.

Over the last year we'd had moments of very strong play, but I think in the matches against Poland, Brazil and then Serbia in the finals, we started defining ourselves as a team so that when the big moment came we would be ready.

Heading into the final against Serbia, we felt like the match we had played against them earlier was a little unfair because we had arrived late. We thought we'd have a much better match-up, even though they are the fifth-ranked team in the world and they are very good. They have one of the best setters, the best opposites and they have three 24-year olds who can fly around and control the ball. They were probably the scariest team that people didn't think of at the Olympics. They are just a difficult team because they are tactically sound and technically sound, and they have a big guy who is not afraid to take the big swings in the big moments.

We felt we had a little bit better strategy the second time. Hugh always says to us that the more we play teams, the harder it is for them to beat us. A lot of teams don't learn from winning or losing against teams, but we think every time we play somebody we know their tendencies more, our scouting reports are better and we're real good at making adjustments. The other teams may just play their style regardless, but we adapt to whatever gives us the best chance to have some success. I think our aggressive play got us that victory as we won 3-1.

I was lucky enough to be named the MVP of the tournament, and the only real nice thing about it is I can afford the new furniture my wife just bought. It could have gone to Clay, it could have gone to Reid… You could have picked four guys out of our starting six who were the MVP. I was fine, good enough to get the team where it needed to go. Since I've been back, I know people have been saying I've been playing my best volleyball, not because I've been great, but I think now if you look back over the last two years, you'd be hard-pressed to say there was a match where you could say, "Lloy was bad." That's what I wanted to change. I wanted to make sure I was good every night, and that sometimes means you'll have a little up or a little down, but if you are just good every night in our sport, that wins a lot of matches.

I was happy about being named the MVP, but I could have handed it anyone and have been just as happy.

I didn't feel redeemed or anything like that because we won the World League title. The European Champions League and the Olympics are in my opinion the two premier events in volleyball. It's the pinnacle of club play and the pinnacle of national team play. Giba doesn't have a Champions League title, Karch doesn't have that title. Obviously, the Italian championships, the Greek championships and the Russian championships are awesome, but if someone asked me what I'd like to be remembered for in my career it would be winning the gold medal and winning champions league.

CHAPTER 39

This team didn't have near as many cliques as some teams will have, though you are obviously closer with some guys than others. When we got between the white lines, it was anything to help your teammates.

There weren't a lot of dinners between Reid Priddy and me, though we did become a lot closer. Ryan Millar and I don't go to movies together. I like hang out with Sean Rooney or Clay better, but guys never let the petty little differences come through which can sometimes destroy teams. We were not going to let that be the reason we didn't win. Whenever we stepped on the court, it was whatever we could do, whatever I could do to help the guy next to you.

If you look back since World League, as soon as Clay went bad, Reid picked him up. When Reid went bad, David blocked a ball. When Lee couldn't block, I made a dig. You can't say that with Russia where the opposite carried them, or with Brazil and Giba. Eventually those guys are going to fail, and they aren't going to have a great game. If you look at our stat sheet after the World League matches or the Olympic matches, we wouldn't have a guy other than Clay once in a while with more than 20 kills. We'd have four guys with 14 to 16 kills. If I'm the other team's coach and I'm trying to tell my guys where to block, where do I send them?

After the World League, I think our expectations grew from we could be on the podium to if we're not on podium it's going to be a disappointment. I don't think our expectations went to, "Hey, it's gold medal time." I remember saying as we were on our way to Beijing that anything less than being on the podium would be disappointing for this team. At the beginning, I'd always says if we play the best we can and we don't have what it takes, then so be it, but by then we knew the best we could put out there was podium material.

CHAPTER 40

After winning the World League title, we went home to Anaheim for a couple days, but we got into Beijing on August 3 to get used to the 12-hour time change. We also felt the longer we stayed in Anaheim with everyone's friends and families the more the distractions would be. We got acclimated in part by practicing in all the venues we were going to play in. Despite that, those were the longest five days ever. I could not wait to start playing. We've been training for this, in my case, for 15 years and it was like, enough, let's strap this on and see what happens.

The opening ceremonies were on August 8, and four of us didn't march, Stanley, Hoff, Salmon and I. The young guys asked me about it, and I said, "Shoot, this is your first Olympics, you get out there and put the uniform on – even though you're going to look retarded and you're going to sweat – and march because it's something you're going to remember the rest of your life." Knowing that it was my last Olympics, I'd have liked to have gone, but I just knew that I'd still have felt it when we played two days later.

People don't realize the ceremonies start at 8 p.m., but that means we show up at 3 p.m., stand around for five hours in our polo suits in 95-degree heat. Then you get into the infield, and there's no seating there and there are no water bottles. After all that, people are destroyed for days. As awesome as it is, it's not something that a 36-year old athlete who is serious about winning a gold medal probably needs to do.

The village was great, the best one I've been to. It was set up where there were two apartments with three bedrooms each, and they were big rooms with air conditioning. The TV had CNN, HBO and live feeds of all the events. It was all-USA in our building and we had all our medical staff on the bottom floor so they were all there for our treatments. The second floor was all computers and phones to call home for free. The village was huge, but it was only a 10-minute walk to anywhere or you could buy bicycles for $50 and ride those around if you wanted to. The food was relatively good. It was like a glorified dorm at a nice university. Whoever ends up buying those places will be real pleased because they are nice.

There was one kind of uncomfortable moment. I was sitting at a computer and a girl sat down next to me, a tall blond, so I look over and it's Amy Cuff, the high jumper who posed in Playboy. I said hi and she said hi. So I'm typing away and another girl comes and sits down to the left of me, and I look over and it's Amanda Beard who also posed in Playboy. I was thinking to myself, "If my wife walked in right now, I wonder how she'd view this whole situation?" That was kind of funny, but I didn't strike up a conversation about it.

The men's and women's basketball team trained right before and after us, so Kobe was always coming in and talking to us and came to two of our matches. They seemed like any other athletes. The women were always friendly. I didn't go out of my way a lot this time to meet people. I made sure to say hi to Dirk Nowitzki and Manu Ginobili because I'm a basketball fan. It's an amazing scene, and it still surprises me even though it's my fourth Olympics. You're sitting there in the mess hall eating with your buddies, and you see guys like that walk by with Germany on or an Argentina shirt on, or you see Michael Phelps in line at McDonald's. Even we get a little gawky because those guys are superstars. It's still cool. I'll definitely remember getting to say hi to those people.

This is the most focused I've ever been, partly – and I joke about it but it's true – because I'm so tired. I basically have like six hours a day to give. I'm just tired because I've been playing a long time and I'm a dad. As most dads know, there's no "off" switch – kids go until they can't go and then you try to talk to your wife for a half hour before you fall asleep and it starts all over again at 5 a.m. I just didn't have a lot of energy for all the extra stuff.

CHAPTER 41

The day before we were to play Venezuela, on August 9, we're training at Beijing Normal University, and about halfway through practice coach Hugh McCutcheon grabs his bag and leaves. I'm thinking it's probably another media thing or something like that because he gets called away all the time for gosh knows what. After practice, you could tell the mood of the staff was kind of somber, and Rob Browning our team leader says we were going to have a meeting after we showered. Right then we knew it wasn't good news. Everyone was kind of hoping it wasn't someone from back home.

We get into the room and Kerry Klostermann, the Secretary General of USA Volleyball, comes in and says there's been an incident with Hugh's family. Then he goes on to explain how the Bachmans and Wiz, Hugh's wife, were attacked. Todd Bachman was killed and they don't know how Barbara is. The police wouldn't let Hugh even get close to them at first.

It was all so vague what happened. Of course everyone, and I was one of the worst, had a huge knee-jerk reaction. When they are telling me this, the whole time I'm thinking, five hours from now my family is getting on a plane to come over. I was like, "Screw that, they're not coming."

The first thing they wanted us to do was to call home even though it was 3 or 4 in the morning because they knew the news would break soon and it would be vague, and they didn't want our families to think it was one of us. Sure enough, the first headline on CNN was "Member of volleyball delegation was injured," which was as vague as it could possibly be.

I called Mom and Dad first at 4 a.m., to give Sarah a little more time to sleep and to let them know what was happening. I thought they'd be less freaked out, but Dad was pretty concerned, as was Mom. I said, ``Think about it, and I'm going to call Sarah now. I'm going to talk to her and have her call you. You guys talk about it and then together we'll make a decision what's best for everybody." I told Mom and Dad, "There's no way Sarah's coming. With Dyer? Are you kidding me?"

As usual, I was wrong about my wife.

She was like, "Well, we're coming."

I was like, "What?"

"Lloy, people get murdered in Fort Wayne every day, but we still go to Coney Island once a week and don't worry about it. We still go to Wal-Mart, we still do everyday things we need to do to live. As long as we know it's not an act of terrorism against Americans or against men's volleyball or whatever, we're coming. Why wouldn't we come there? You can't live your life in fear, and I want Dyer to see your fourth Olympics. If I feel unsafe in any way at any time there's a plane that goes the other way, too. We're coming."

She called Mom and Dad and talked them back into it. I talked to them both again, and we decided, OK, let's do it.

I told Sarah I was fine with that, but I told her that, "At any point and time, you feel unsafe or I can't get a hold of you, I'm sending you home. I'm here for this, and as much as I love you, I don't want to be thinking all the time about your safety." That was one of the great things about having my friend Lance Adams come along is that he could kind of control everything and take charge of stuff.

They got on the plane and came and everything was fine.

A lot of people felt that what happened to Hugh's family was our motivation for the whole Olympics, and it honestly wasn't, but I think it was a big part of our first match against Venezuela. It could have gone either way and ended up going five games. We came out with their names on our shoes, and we decided to have a little huddle before the match. I think Tom Hoff and Reid Priddy came up with the idea. After we shook hands with Venezuela, we took a quick moment to just kind of gather our thoughts. It was the first time we had played a match without Hugh, and it was on a lot of people's minds so we decided to try to take 30 seconds and put it out of our heads before the match started. It was a moment for each of us to kind of compartmentalize that situation and take it and put it outside the circle and leave it there for now.

It worked. I don't think the guys thought about it, and they came out and played two great sets. Then when we went into the third set and thought we had it in the bag, guys started slipping a little bit with their focus. Something changed, and then I got hurt.

Halfway through the second set, I could feel my left calf start to tighten up, like a sore muscle. It wasn't a cramp, but I told Aaron Brock our trainer that maybe I should get out because if I kept playing it was going to get worse and maybe pull. At that time it just felt like a strain, and you don't want to come out, but by the same token we're in a pretty good spot up 2-0 in the match. I've had a problem with my calves before where they've been tight or started to stretch and I've pushed it, and then I've had slight tears that take four weeks to fix. I felt like if I bailed out then with therapy and 48 hours to rest I could get back on the horse again.

It didn't work out that way and having to come back in the fifth game didn't help. I looked like Arnie back there serving because I couldn't get my left leg off the ground. I probably just should have used a float serve but I hadn't done it in so long I was afraid I'd hit it under the net. I figured it was best if I just went off one leg and tried to get it in.

Usually other guys will pick it up when we have something like that happen, and even without me, that's a team we should beat. It was a nice moment for me to come back in the fifth and say, "Look, whatever you guys are thinking about, stop because it's not working. Just bust our humps for 15 minutes and think about nothing but volleyball so we can bust this Venezuela team and move on." The guys responded and we got back on course.

I'm sure if anybody looks back at the tapes of the match, nobody is going to say, "Wow, Lloy Ball's play is what won it." It was more me yelling and screaming and getting guys fired up. I told them, "I'm here, but I'm a cheerleader. You guys are going to have to carry me. Pass the ball somewhat close to where I'm standing, and kill it because I'm not going to be running around so much." Sometimes brutal honesty is the best thing, I think.

My calf didn't tear, but I strained it enough where it took me probably 10 days of non-stop therapy between matches to feel like it was somewhat back to normal. I started therapy that night. I was doing everything from massage to ultrasound to stim to laser to shock treatment to putting it in a tub of boiling water to putting it in a tub of ice water – you name it, I was doing it. I had more wires coming out of my body than Robocop.

Whenever I wasn't playing over the next 10 days, it was wrapped. When I was playing, it had neoprene with wasabi sauce on it. It was like Ben Gay but 100 times hotter and it was green like wasabi sauce. Especially with neoprene on top of it, it was so hot that I couldn't feel from my knee to my ankle. It could have been broken or ripped, but it was excruciatingly painful so you don't think about the real pain. I wouldn't recommend it to the young athletes out there.

It was a strange, strange start to the Olympics.

CHAPTER 42

Two days after that we came back to play against Italy, and by about the third game I started to feel pretty good. The guys passed the rock that match, and Italy should have known me better than they played. I felt decent after that match.

After every match, the training staff and I would evaluate, and the day after Italy it felt better than it did the day after Venezuela so it was going in the right direction. I asked about possibly not playing against Bulgaria to rest it, but you could see from the faces of the coaches they didn't want to do that so much. After the Bulgaria match, it felt like it did after the Venezuela match so it went backward.

We always seemed to lose the first game against the good teams. A lot of it is I think this team tries to size up our opponents. Sometimes these other teams will just mail it in and sometimes we'll start out wondering, "Who are we getting today? Are we getting the good Italians or the bad Italians?" If it's the bad Italians, we don't have to work that hard to win. A lot of times, by the time we figure out these are the good Italians, we've just lost the first set. It shouldn't be like that, but it was just one of the characteristics of this team. Once we figure it out, then we're in.

After Bulgaria, the coaches wanted me to play against China. They thought China was a good team, we had lost to them earlier in the summer and they were going to be playing at home. I wanted to play the last match against Japan because I didn't want to play China and then have four days off before we play a knockout match. I didn't want to be rusty and I wanted to have some rhythm going into the quarterfinals. I sat out and sure enough, China mailed it in. Those four days were the determining factor that allowed me to play well the next four matches. Had we not done it that way, it would have been tough for me to play at a high level the next few matches.

Another thing that happened was Hugh came back against China. He was a little weird for that one. In the media we talked about how seamless it was, but he was anxious and nervous and uncomfortable. He didn't stay in the village after the attack so he had to meet us for practice or meet us for video. Right there, it's already weird where he's not around the corner if we need to talk to him. You could tell, and I'm sure he may say otherwise, but he wasn't 100 percent that first match. How could he be? Coming back from any kind of tragedy is never easy. Luckily, the game wasn't too difficult. By the next game against Japan he was back on his game.

It was just something that had to be done to get us to the finish line, and it was better that we did it in that match to get him over that hump and us over that hump and me over my injury hump. People will look at that match as insignificant because we won and it was easy, but it was real significant for a lot of people for a lot of reasons.

Before the Japan match Hugh asked me what I wanted to do, and I said a set and a half, two sets if it goes well. After the second set, he was like, "You want to play the third?" I was, "Nope," and he said all right. Kevin Hansen went in and we finished them off. Clay got a breather and some other guys got some rest, and the bench played great. It was another great job by Hugh and the staff of managing us and giving us what we needed at that time. We were the No. 1 seed, and we were all healthy going into the quarters.

That was the best my leg felt from the first set of the Olympics.

Going into the quarterfinals, I think we were the most nervous we were for any match in the Olympics. For one, we knew how good Serbia was. They aren't like a Russia team that may not show up. They are going to show up, and they are going to fight, and they are going to cover a ball with their head or kick one from the stands. You just knew it was going to be a battle. Overriding that is you know if you lose you go home.

And then we lost the first set. Then we were down 2-1 heading into the fourth game and then we were down 7-4 in the fifth game. It was just strange how throughout the match, we found a way to win even through the anxiety. It was a grind it out match where luckily our heart and perseverance paid off in the end. Guys kept finding other ways to help us win. This wasn't the best match we played, but up to that point it was the biggest win of my Olympic career. We won this match because we were a team all the way through.

CHAPTER 43

During the Olympics, I said this was the best team I had played on with the U.S. I'm not sure we had the best volleyball players, but it was the best team collectively. The guys all played real hard for each other, and we tried to continually push if we were ahead or behind. If one guy wasn't playing well, the other guys tried to pick him up. It was definitely the most cohesive group that been on in the Olympics.

Here's a little bit about my teammates who started in the Olympics.

Clay Stanley: Had Clay not have been on the national team, I don't think I would have pursued it so strongly. I think he's become the most dominant opposite in the world. I know people talk about his serve and his attack, but he won a lot of matches for us with his blocking, with his finesse shots that he's not known for, and for his positive attitude and not getting his head down like he used to in the past. He's become the real deal. I've played with him for eight years, and he's never once complained to me. I know he's going to work hard for me. As we've shown the last three or four years, we're the most dominant setter-opposite combination in the world.

Reid Priddy: He's the best athlete the U.S. has had on the team since Karch Kiraly. As he's matured, he's getting the mental take of Karch as well. I think he'll be even better in the next Olympics. He's a guy who is going to be physically great for the next eight years, and now his mental game has caught up to his physicality. It was hard for us originally because he was the show, he was the guy getting 30 sets for our team before I showed up, and he was the guy on all the posters. He was the guy people talked about for all the spectacular things he does, and I think it was a big step for our team when he allowed his role to diminish to become a guy who was getting 20 sets a match. He was not going to be allowed to do whatever he wants, but he was going to pass the ball and play within a team system. To his credit, he let that happen, and his maturation was a huge, huge part of our success.

Riley Salmon: At the World Cup in 2006, he woke the sleeping giant of Russia by screaming through the net and we ended up losing. He was so focused in this tournament. He was never out, never had a casual beer for dinner, he was always watching extra video and he kept his mouth shut against Italy and Russia when you know he wanted to open it. He looked at me when he knows I haven't set him in a while and we're struggling, knowing he wants to say, "Hey, dumb ass, set me," but he didn't. He's only 6-2, and he's been fighting the little man syndrome his whole life, and he's blocking balls for us and digging and no one had bigger kills in the semifinals than he did. I'm just real happy for him and all that he's gone through. He came from Pierce Junior College in Texas. He might as well be from Indiana as far as volleyball goes. Everyone saying he's not big enough and not strong enough, but here he is a gold medalist. He was just another huge part of our team.

Rich Lambourne: Rich is a guy who I have sometimes wanted to kill. It just seemed like in every fifth set he'd shank a ball at a very important time. A couple of years ago I would have ripped his head off, but he did a very nice job of keeping his cool and his next ball he'd pass perfectly or he'd make a huge dig. While I don't think he's the best defensive Libero ever or the best passing Libero ever, he's just a nice fit for our team. He didn't cause waves the way Erik Sullivan did in the past, though Sullivan is my boy. Rich doesn't say much, which is good and bad, but he goes methodically about his job and you know exactly what you are going to get from him. He's always going to be good. The key to that position is being mentally strong, which he is. He does a nice job handling that pressure, and his demeanor is what it needs to be to be a great Libero.

Ryan Millar: I was real happy for him because he's been around a long time, too. This was his third Olympics, and he's a little undersized, if you really think about it. He's only 6-6, maybe 6-7 compared to the 6-10 Russian middles who can touch 12 feet. He's always been a great blocker and offensively he was awesome during the Olympics. As you want all hitters to be, he has always wanted the ball. When he didn't get the ball, he always complained about it, but this time he put a lot of trust in me. When I wasn't setting him in some games, he would do other things. When I was able to set him, he did a great job. I think from the beginning of the tournament, people know I like to set middle and they know Ryan and I have played together a long time. Where they didn't commit to Dave because they weren't sure, they gave Ryan a lot of respect.

David Lee: I love Dave Lee. He may not take this as a compliment, and I'm not sure it is, he's a young Lloy Ball but a lot better as a player. I've never seen a guy who lives life in a good and bad way, but he lives for that court. He lives to compete and take that ball and shove it right down your throat and then tell you about it. He's not afraid of anybody. He's not a huge guy, but he's quick and smart. Blocking, I've never seen a guy read a setter so quick and react. He's a guy you can motivate. Once at the World League we were playing against Brazil, and he's not blocking anything so I get Tom Hoff off the bench and walk him right in front of Dave during a time out. "Tom, are you ready to play because we need someone who can block a ball?" Lee looks at me and says something unprintable and goes out and stuffs about four of the next five. In the Olympics we're playing Russia and he's been great offensively, but I'm looking at him, and he's like "What? You've been looking at me all night." And I say, "I've been waiting about two hours for you to block a damn ball. I'm tired of trying to dig them all back here." He gets mad and goes out and scores the last five points for us. So, I've got David Lee down. He has a real bright future.

CHAPTER 44

We had a bone to pick with Russia in the semifinals. We hadn't beaten Russian in an FIVB event since 1993, a streak of nine straight matches. They had knocked us out of qualifying at the World Cup and had knocked us out of the bronze medal at the last Olympics so we were pretty anxious to beat them. Clay and I played with their two outsides the last two years in Kazan and see them every day in Russia. We also play against all the rest of those guys in the Russian league.

That was one match where we came out ready to play right from the start. We were up 2-0 and if it wasn't for that 19-year old opposite they got from Siberia, it should have been a 3-0 match. He decided to get 50 points, and only after the David Lee conversation did he decide to stop him.

That was the most fun match I've played in the Olympics. Even winning the goal medal wasn't as fun as the Russian match. There were a lot of underlying reasons, such as knowing we played so well against a team that we struggled with in the past and knowing we were going to win a medal. There was also knowing for the next year I could walk around Russia with my shoulders back, not having to have my head down. It would have been lot tougher to play there if we had lost.

There was also getting to share it with Sarah and Dyer and Mom and Dad. Sarah was crying, and Dyer was all red in the face from cheering and screaming all night. That day after the Russia match was the first time I actually left the village to spend an hour with them. This was a moment I wanted to remember for at least an hour.

I really thought that after the Russia match the guys would be all loosey/ goosey for the gold medal match against Brazil. We were guaranteed to get a medal so let's just go and play and see what happens. But guys were pretty anxious again because they thought we could win. That's when anxiety and nerves come back and we started slow.

I really wasn't that nervous because I thought we would win. I didn't think it would be 3-0 because ever since Serbia, I just expected them all to be five-game matches. As most final matches go, if people really think about it, they aren't the prettiest volleyball matches. Both teams are nervous, it's the biggest stage in the world and errors are amplified by the spectators. I thought we did the best job of just managing the situations. When we needed a couple of key digs, we made them. When we needed some blocks, we got them. We didn't serve gangbusters, or pass fantastically well, but if you look at the stats we made about 20 percent fewer errors than they did.

I can tell you the exact moment I knew we were going to win. It came late in the fourth game and we were down 20-17. The ball was rolled over by Dante, and the blockers tried to stay down, but it hit Stanley's head and went over and fell down. I just knew it was going to work out. Sure, enough, Giba hits the next ball out of bounds and then we make a dig and get a kill to tie it.

After match point, even though it was probably three seconds of real time, I seriously had about 30 minutes of things go through my head, from I want to run to my family right now, to Oh, I can't run because that would look really bad because I should stay and celebrate with my team right now, to, I can't believe it took me 12 years to get here, to I'm sure everyone at home is watching and I'm so happy they supported me, to I can't believe my national career is over, to I can't believe it finally happened, to I wish my daughter was here, to I'm glad my son is here, to I'm so lucky… it just went on and on. Every thought I've had in my while career went through my head in three seconds.

Finally, the guys mobbed me and it was tears and hugging. That went on for probably five minutes, and then I snapped around and went over and jumped the barricade and went over to where Sarah was. She was in tears. Lance was crying, Mom and Dad were crying. Dyer was just jumping up and down. I just hugged and hugged. My dad said something and I can't even remember what he said. It was just overwhelming that it was all over – everything, the match, the journey, the striving for the medal, the years of training.

It's funny I guess when you strive for something for years in business, athletics or whatever, it pushes your life every day in everything you do, from training and eating and sleeping and where you live, to when do you have surgery, do we try to have a kid now because if we do I won't be around here and then… and then when that one thing that determined your life for 20 years is accomplished, it's almost bittersweet. As I was on the bus going to the party, I thought about I didn't know what to do. Did I even want to play volleyball any more? I felt lost, even though I was happy at the same time. I was so elated but also so confused.

The guys kept saying they were so happy for me, and they kept asking me if I was happy. I was, but it was different. I was so happy I wanted to cry, but I was like, I can't let it out. It was a little strange. I've had a couple of moments since then by myself where it's kind of hit me. I thought back to Sydney when we lost to Korea to fall to 0-5 and my knee is throbbing and I'm going to have to have surgery, and I'm sitting there with Doug Beal crying, thinking it's over and it didn't happen. Then four years later in Athens, I remember after we lost the bronze medal match, sitting in the shower by myself crying because I wasn't going to play any more. I had kind of been through that a couple of times, but I didn't know how to react. If we had lost, I knew how to react because it had happened before. We didn't lose, which was a good thing, but I didn't know how to react to winning.

I was just kind of at a loss for words and actions, which for me is difficult.

When we were standing on the podium and they were coming down with the medals, I saw that Bob Ctvrtlik was going to end up being the guy to put the medal on me. Bob had been my teammate in 1996 in Atlanta when I started this journey and now he's one of three Americans on the International Olympic Committee. The first thing I thought of is, he may say, "Hey, you son of a gun, why didn't you win one for me in 1996?" But I could tell by the look on his face and by the fact that he and his wife Cosse and kids were at the last three matches yelling louder than anybody that he was happy for me. She even went to talk to Sarah after one match and said, "It's so funny because now you guys are what we were when Lloy first joined the team, the old couple with the kids. In a couple of years you and Lloy will be what Bob and I are up here in the stands." Leave it to an athlete's wife to put a reality check on it.

To have Bob put it around my neck... People talk about Karch and Steve Timmons and Jeff Stork, but to me Ctvrtlik is my guy. He had nowhere near the athletic ability of Karch, but he made himself one of the three greatest passers we've ever had, and he's for sure one of the fiercest competitors we've ever had. He's a great role model as a man and as a player. When I think of USA Volleyball, I think of Bob, and to have him put the gold medal around my neck is better than Bush, it was better than if Jordan had done it or anyone else they could have gotten. It just meant that much more to me. They all smile and shake your hand, but we had a real moment there that I know I'll tell my grandkids about. He just said, "It finally happened. I knew it would. You just needed it to be your time, and this is your time."

CHAPTER 45

As I look back on my career, and it's kind of in two parts, the pre-kid part and the post-kid part.

The pre-kid part was a lot of fun. I had a lot more energy, I got a lot more sleep and a lot more attention from my wife. Then all of a sudden I turned 28 and my wife gets pregnant while we're in Italy. We have the ultrasound and see that it's going to be a boy, and I just start crying. Every father loves their kids, boys or girls, but every father would say it's a huge deal to have your first kid be a boy.

I couldn't wait to call my dad. I remember talking to he and Mom on the phone and I'm crying and I tell them that we're pregnant and it's a boy, and I can hear my dad swallow as hard as a man can swallow. It was one of the happier moments of my life.

All of a sudden I have a kid, and I'm sleeping four hours a night and I'm not training nearly as hard so I put on a couple of pounds, but somehow I start playing better. I'm playing hard in practice, but quicker so I can get home to see the wife and kid. For some reason in every match I don't feel quite as nervous. I'm tired, but I can feel there's slowly becoming a different kind of balance in my life. That's what the kids did for me. They put things in perspective for me.

No matter how cool junior girls volleyball players think you are, no matter how many covers of Seventeen magazine or Volleyball Monthly you are on, having your kid run out to you on the court after a match or having them run to the front door when you come home after practice is better than anything. I remember after matches in Modena, for example, I'd be exhausted and Dyer would waddle out there at age three and want to get the ball and play on the court. The coach would be like, "Hey, go ice your knees. We've got another game coming up." And I'd be like, "I'm going to play with my kid." I always found time and energy to roll the ball with him, or to pick him up so he could throw it over the net. Or in Greece when he was old enough, he wanted to bump after the match. Then he wants to go to the gym with Dad.

He was slowly becoming the little man that I became to Arnie. The father-son relationship that my dad had that grew into a friendship is every father's dream. This Olympics is the perfect example. I talked to him every day all summer and at the Olympics, and all he wanted to know was when was I coming over to the apartment. Sarah would be like, "Tell Daddy how good he played," and Dyer would be like, "Dad you played great. When are you coming over?" He wanted to play or wrestle because Grandpa is too old, or Mommy is too weak, only Daddy can wrestle him. Only Daddy can make up good board games off the top of his head that include the action figures and dice and a deck of cards.

I told a reporter at the Olympics, "It makes you appreciate what's real important in life – not necessarily playing in the Olympics, but that your son thinks you're so cool that he shares his action figures with you." My son thinking that I'm a cool guy he likes spending time with is better than any gold medal. The gold medal is something people are going to forget about. Ten years from now they aren't going to have Lloy Ball Day, but hopefully my kid still wants me to play catch with him, and hopefully coach his team.

That's what I remember about my dad. I can't tell you anything my dad ever won, and he had a trophy case as big as a room, but I can tell when he brought a first baseman's glove home and we made a homemade plate and he let me pitch to him. I can tell you how he talked me down one year when our championship T-Ball game got canceled and I was so upset, and I can tell you about a million other things. I think those are memories are probably things he cherishes, too, as opposed to games he played.

Athletics, as awesome as they are, especially in this country with the pedestal we put our athletes on, in the end, it's just really posturing, it's just really trying to make a living. I'm not saying winning a gold medal isn't important because it is. It's what I've been working for my whole life, but it's more important the life it has given me that I can give my family and the time I'm allowed to spend with them. In the end my son wanting to spend time with me because he thinks I'm worth it is the most important thing to me.

It basically all comes down to action figures.

About the authors

Lloy Ball played in his fourth Olympics in August 2008 as a member of the gold medal-winning United States men's volleyball team. A native of Woodburn, Indiana, and a former all-American at IPFW, he and his wife Sarah have a son, Dyer, and a daughter, Mya. Ball has played more than 400 matches with the U.S. national team and was the squad's captain for 10 years.

Blake Sebring has been a sportswriter for the Fort Wayne, Indiana, News-Sentinel for 25 years and is also the author of ``Tales of the Komets,'' ``Legends of the Komets'' and co-author of the upcoming ``Live from Radio Rinkside: The Bob Chase story.''

Printed in the United States
137688LV00003B/1/P